Pastoral Counseling and Personality Disorders

A Manual

Richard P. Vaughan, S.J., Ph.D.

Sheed & Ward

Imprimi Potest
Rev. Paul F. Belcher, S.J.
Provincial, California Province of the Society of Jesus

Sheed & Ward™ is a service of The National Catholic Reporter Pub-
lishing Company.

Library of Congress Cataloguing in Publication Data

Vaughan, Richard P. (Richard Patrick), 1919-
    Pastoral counseling and personality disorders : a manual /
Richard P. Vaughan.
        p.   cm.
    Includes bibliographical references and index.
    ISBN 1-55612-660-3 (alk. paper)
        1. Pastoral counseling. 2. Personality disorders—Religious aspects
—Christianity. 3. Personality disorders—Patients—Pastoral
counseling of. 4. Personality disorders—Patients—Religious life.
5. Church work with the mentally ill.   I. Title.
BV4012.2.V383 1994
253.5′2—dc20   93-36373
                                                                CIP

Published by: Sheed & Ward
                 115 E. Armour Blvd.
                 P.O. Box 419492
                 Kansas City, MO 64141

To order, call: (800) 333-7373

Contents

List of Tables

Dedicated to the late Henry Yoshioka, S.J.
whose technical assistance allowed me to complete
this project and to whom I am deeply indebted.

Acknowledgments

Part of Chapter 1: Introduction was originally published in "Growing in Christian Faith," in *Human Development*, Vol. 5, No. 3, Fall 1984. Reprinted with permission.

Items from *The Harvard Mental Health Review* and *The Harvard Medical School Mental Health Letter* reprinted with permission from *The Harvard Mental Health Review*.

Items from *Disorders of Personality*; DSM-III-R, Axis II, by Theodore Millon, ©1981, reprinted by permission of John Wiley & Sons, Inc.

Diagnostic criteria for personality disorders (see List of Tables) reprinted from American Psychiatric Association: *Diagnostic and Statistical Manual of Mental Disorders, Third Edition, Revised*, Washington, DC, American Psychiatric Association, 1987. Reprinted by permission.

Table 12 is taken from *Depression: The Facts*, by George Winokur, with permission of the Oxford University Press.

Preface

OVER THE PAST 25 YEARS AS A PRIEST AND PSYCHOLOGIST, I HAVE engaged in a variety of counseling situations: pastoral counseling, spiritual direction, psychological counseling and psychotherapy. One evening not too long ago, I reflected upon the large number of people I had seen over the years, coming from every walk of life, ranging in age from 18 to almost 80; and I realized that many of these people suffered, to some degree, from one or another personality disorder. For some the disorder was only mildly handicapping but for others it seriously interfered with just about every aspect of their lives.

At the time, it struck me that if pastoral counselors (or anyone else dealing with people in a church setting) are to be effective in their ministry, they need to be aware of the various types of personality disorders they may encounter, how these disorders hinder people from fully living their lives of faith, and how they as pastoral counselors should deal with people who have these disorders.

The purpose of this book is not to teach pastoral counselors how to be psychological counselors but rather how to be effective pastoral counselors. Personality disorders can and do disrupt both religious belief and its practice. It is my hope that pastoral counselors who read this book will become more aware of the personality disorders in the people they see, more understanding of these individuals, and, as a consequence, better able to help them lead fuller lives of faith and solve their personal problems according to the message of the Gospel.

Even though this work is written by a Catholic priest and sometimes uses specifically Catholic terminology, I think that all Christian pastoral counselors who have faith in Jesus Christ and the Gospel message will profit from what this book has to offer. Inasmuch as spiritual direction and pastoral counseling are considered by some to be essentially the same process, or at least to overlap in the kinds of people and problems they deal with, spiritual directors should also find the pages of this book profitable reading. Also, this book offers psychiatrists, psychologists, social workers, and marriage and family counselors the opportunity to attain a fuller understanding of the part religion plays in the lives of those patients or clients who have a personality disorder.

In each of the chapters on a specific personality disorder, there is a section that deals with the religious beliefs and practices of people with that particular disorder. Most of the material given in these sections come from my own experience in caring for people with a specific disorder.

Each chapter treating a personality disorder or disorders begins with a brief case history which describes the behavior of an individual with a particular personality disorder. For the most part, these cases are taken from my own experience in psychotherapy, psychological counseling or pastoral counseling. To insure confidentiality, I have changed some of the details and circumstances in each of these cases. In a couple of instances, I was unable to recall having treated a person with a particular personality disorder, or the cases I could recall were not suitable. In these instances, I have taken cases from *DSM-III Case Book*, by Robert L. Spitzer et al, published by the American Psychiatric Association, to exemplify a particular personality disorder. Each of the cases gives the reader a concrete example of how a person with a particular personality disorder thinks, feels, and acts.

I wish to express my gratitude to Gerdenio M. Manuel, S.J., whose suggestions have greatly enhanced this project, to Robert V. Caro, S.J., for his meticulous editorial work, and to the late Henry H. Yoshioka, S.J., for his technical assistance in producing the manuscript.

Richard P. Vaughan, S.J.

CHAPTER ONE

Introduction

EACH PERSON WHO SEEKS PASTORAL COUNSELING HAS A UNIQUE personality that affects in some way his or her religious belief and the practice of that belief. Personality can be normal or abnormal, ordered or disordered. This book deals primarily with the disordered personality and its effect upon an individual's religious belief and spiritual life.

The term "personality" refers to a consistent and enduring pattern of thinking, feeling and acting that influences in some way almost every aspect of an individual's life. We all develop our own way of looking at the world, our own attitude toward that world, and our own particular way of acting, all of which go into the making of our personalities. "The idea of personality implies that people's attitudes and behavior differ characteristically in ways that persist through changing situations and over long periods of time. These traits or habits are assumed to be largely unconscious approaches to the world expressed in everything a person thinks, feels, and does."[1]

Personality can be normal or abnormal, well-ordered or disordered, well-functioning or malfunctioning. If the personality is normal, well-ordered and well-functioning, it allows the individual to think, feel and act in a harmonious, balanced and efficient way. If, however, the personality is abnormal, disordered, or malfunctioning, then the person's way of thinking, feeling and acting is often distorted, confused and even chaotic; such an individual is said to have a personality disorder.[2] If he or she is a person of faith, then the personality disorder can adversely affect his or her faith.

1

Religion and the Disordered Personality

People with normal personalities are more apt to be balanced in their religious convictions and practice, whereas people with disordered personalities are more likely to misunderstand or misinterpret some of their religious beliefs, sometimes engaging in extreme or unusual religious practices. They may also have faulty attitudes about their religious beliefs and find that the disorder interferes with putting into practice what they believe. For example, a man with a schizoid personality disorder, who usually has great difficulty relating to others and forming any kind of an emotional attachment to another person, is likely to have the same difficulty when he tries to relate to God in prayer. Or an obsessive-compulsive woman may see herself as sinning at times when there is no sin. She may be driven to overcome her guilt feelings by confessing her sins repeatedly, sometimes as often as three times in the same afternoon, because she is never sure that she has accurately described her sins to the confessor and received forgiveness.

Evaluating the Counselee

Those who engage in pastoral counseling need to consider both the extent of the person's faith and his or her personality type. If there is any indication of a disordered personality, the pastoral counselor should try to determine where the person stands on the continuum between normal and abnormal, well-ordered and disordered, well-functioning and malfunctioning, and then adapt the counseling process to fit the personality and faith of the individual.

Usually people with healthy personalities function well in almost every sector of their lives, whether at work, home, church, or in social situations. By contrast, those with disordered personalities find themselves unable to get along well with other people or to work productively. Indeed, they live in a state of considerable inner emotional turmoil, no matter where they are. How the person functions in different environments, and his or her persistent emotional state constitute criteria whereby the pastoral counselor can judge whether the person has a healthy or unhealthy personality. If experienced over an extended period of time, such tension and distress may have an effect upon the individual's attitude toward religion and the practice of his or her faith.

Purpose of the Book

This book deals with the various types of personality disorders, as well as a few of the more common psychotic conditions sometimes encountered by pastoral counselors. It offers practical ideas on how pastoral counselors can help people with one of these personality disorders so the disorder interferes as little as possible with their faith and the practice of that faith.

The aim is not to show pastoral counselors how to do psychological counseling or psychotherapy since these techniques are the functions of psychiatrists and clinical psychologists and demand special knowledge and extensive training, far beyond the book's scope. However, the book offers pastoral counselors some basic skills and techniques used by psychiatrists or psychologists that may be helpful in assisting people to live their faith according to the Gospel message and resolve their problems in the light of that message.

Classifying Mental Conditions

Mental conditions are classified under a number of distinct categories that often are not as sharply delineated from each other as psychiatrists or psychologists would like. Nonetheless, these classifications give professionals a way of describing abnormal behavior so they can make a diagnosis and conduct research. They also give professional people a vocabulary to discuss with each other the many mental and emotional conditions that plague the human race.

Personality disorders are just one of several classifications of abnormal behavior. The other major classifications are organic (disorder of physiological origin), psychotic (withdrawal from reality and intellectual, emotional, and social malfunctioning), and neurotic conditions (psychological condition with fear, anxiety and inability to cope). Until quite recently, personality disorders were listed under one of the other classifications, usually as some kind of a neurotic condition, which is due to an unconscious inner conflict, rather than to faulty personality development. DSM-III-R has also broken down the neurotic condition into more concrete classifications.

System of Classification

The system of classification used in this book is the *Diagnostic and Statistical Manual* (DSM-III-R), which is commonly used by psychiatrists and psychologists in the United States. The DSM-III-R was constructed by the American Psychiatric Association and has gone through four revisions since 1952, when the first edition appeared.[3] As the body of psychiatric and psychological knowledge grew, psychiatrists reevaluated the validity of old classifications in the first and each subsequent edition. They excluded listings they found no longer accurate and devised new categories and classifications based on more recent research.

Summary Tables

Summary tables of the major behavior characteristics for each of the personality disorders are taken from DSM-III-R. If an individual manifests approximately three-quarters of the behavior patterns listed in a table, he or she is thought to have that particular personality disorder. In some cases, the tables have been simplified by translating technical terminology into more commonly-understood language, but the tables are substantially the same as those in DSM-III-R.

Meaning of Religion

Because religion assumes such a wide variety of forms, it is difficult to define. For Christians, however, religion means belief in God as creator and governor of the universe, and in Jesus Christ and what Jesus Christ has taught. In Christianity what is believed about God and the supernatural world has been revealed through the prophets of the Old Testament, such as Jeremiah, Isaiah, Ezekiel, and finally through Jesus Christ and the ongoing tradition of the Church. "In times past God spoke in partial and various ways to our ancestors through the prophets; in these last days, He spoke to us through a Son, whom He made heir of all things and through whom He created the universe" (Hebrews 1, 1-2). This revelation contains what God has said to His people and is the basis of Christian faith. What we know about God and His world is made known to us through revelation, which Christians accept as true. It is our faith that allows us to believe what God has revealed to us.

What is Faith?

When one thinks of faith, what usually comes to mind is a set of beliefs, such as those found in the Nicene or Apostles' Creed, but faith is much more than a set of beliefs. Faith is an enduring state of the *whole person* that involves intellectual assent, willing, trust, relationship, and commitment. Vatican II states: "The obedience of faith must be given to God who reveals, an obedience by which one entrusts one's whole self freely to God, offering the full submission of the intellect and will to God who reveals, and freely assenting to the revelation given him."[4] Faith, therefore, means accepting with one's whole being something on the word of God *rather than on the basis of one's own direct experience.*

There are two ways of knowing something: 1) by direct experience, and 2) by the word of another. You know your neighbor next door because you have met and talked with him over the back fence many times, whereas your knowledge of Mother Teresa is dependent upon reports from newspapers and magazine articles which you have read and accepted as true. Much of what we know is based on natural faith. We accept it because we trust the veracity of its source.

Christian Faith

Just about every religion is built upon some kind of faith. Christianity is built on faith in Jesus, who is the Risen Christ and the Son of God, and the message Jesus has given us, especially through the Gospels.[5] The core of Jesus's message is the Trinity, namely that God is Father, Son, and Holy Spirit, and upon this message depends our relationship with God and commitment to Christianity.

Faith includes the relationship we have with Jesus, as Son of God and Savior, as well as the acceptance of what Jesus taught. "Christian faith is an encounter with Jesus Christ, who meets the believer through His Spirit, while the believer meets Christ through the gift of faith, which allows the believer to know and accept Christ and the message Christ taught."[6] Our faith allows us to form a trusting relationship with God, confident that God will be faithful to us, even when we have failed to be faithful to Him.

Faith effects a lasting state of mind that allows us to accept what God through Jesus has revealed to us about Himself and His plans for the world.

> What God has revealed is set, but what a particular revealed truth means to an individual can differ from one person to another. We assent to the statement 'We believe in one God, the Father, the Almighty' because we accept it as a revealed truth. The statement itself is constant but what the statement means to a person varies from individual to individual. As a consequence of development, learning and experience, we each have a somewhat different way of looking at God and the content of our faith.[7]

In pastoral counseling the counselor tries to relate the individual's faith to the matter that he or she brings to the counseling session. Consequently, we need to have an understanding of the individual's faith, and then look for ways to utilize that faith in helping the individual cope with his or her problem.

Sharing Our Faith

One of the ways pastoral counselors can help counselees is through sharing their own faith. In the process of faith-sharing, counselors reveal their own faith and Christian values. Sidney Jourard has shown that counselors who talk about their own background and feelings facilitate a similar disclosure by the counselee.[8] When counselors are willing to talk openly about what they believe and treasure, they find that their counselees gain new understanding of their own faith and values, and also that the counselees are more willing to talk about what they believe and how it influences their lives. This, in turn, provides the counselee an opportunity to examine in depth his or her faith commitment.[9]

Christian Values

A value is that which is esteemed, prized, or deemed worthwhile and desirable by a person or culture. Christian values stem from faith in Jesus Christ and the message he taught. Christian faith causes us to look upon certain ways of thinking, acting, and living as worthwhile and desirable; these special ways of thinking, acting, and living constitute a system of Christian values. An example of a Christian value is respect for the human dignity of each person with whom we come in contact, which stems from the commandment Jesus Christ gave us to love our neighbor as ourselves. This Christian value determines how we think, feel, and act in regard to other people, races, and nations, even though we may not like these people and even, at times, consider them enemies. We prize all other human beings because of their dignity as creatures of God and because both we and they have God as a common Source. This respect and love for others is closely linked to the commandment to "love God with all your heart, with all your soul and with all your mind and your neighbor as yourself" (Mt. 22:37). The two commandments are as one and the foundation for all our Christian values.

The Impact of Personality

Belief in God and God's revelation is substantially the same from one Catholic to the next. However, each person's attitude toward that belief, what he or she emphasizes as important, how he or she feels about what is believed, and how he or she relates to God, especially in the person of Jesus Christ, varies, depending upon the condition of the individual's personality. Thus if a person lives amidst great emotional turmoil due to a personality disorder, then faith can be a source of distress and anguish. An example of the influence of a personality on faith can be seen in the woman with an obsessive-compulsive personality disorder who spent hours trying to decide whether she committed a serious sin or not, all the time becoming more and more confused and depressed. She would not experience such distress, or at least not so severely, were she not a believing Christian.

Pastoral Counseling

In pastoral counseling a person of faith tries to help another person (usually of a similar faith) live that faith more fully and solve their problems according to the message of the Gospel.[10] People seek help for a variety of reasons: when they are unable to cope with fears and anxieties, anger, guilt due to interpersonal problems, marital and family conflicts, sexual problems, alcoholism and drug abuse, physical and emotional abuse, and during periods of transition in their lives or at the death or loss of a loved one. Those who seek pastoral counseling need help to cope with personal, social, marital, vocational, or spiritual problems in accordance with their beliefs and values.

They are looking for a special type of counseling, namely one that includes their faith and personal values as essential components in seeking a way to handle what brings them to counseling. At least indirectly, these people also hope that their faith will be enhanced, that their way of living according to the message of the Gospel will be improved by their contact with a pastoral counselor.

What is Counseling?

Counseling is a dialogue in which a counselor attempts to help another person change his or her behavior way of thinking and attitudes, make decisions, solve problems or cope with a variety of life situations so as to maximize opportunities and minimize adverse environmental conditions. The counselor encourages individuals to speak about their thoughts, feelings, and experiences, with the hope that they will come to better understand themselves and their situation, and, as a consequence, feel enabled to make needed changes in their lives. If there is a problem, the counselee is encouraged to consider possible ways to solve the problem, and then to implement the way he or she has chosen.

Who Engages in Pastoral Counseling

Pastoral counseling is one type of counseling. In the past, pastoral counseling was almost exclusively the domain of priests, who frequently had no training for this ministry other than their theological education. Today, most seminaries include some courses in pastoral counseling; moreover, the counseling ministry has been opened to others, such as sisters, brothers and the laity, who have also usually received some training. At present there are a number of church organizations that use lay pastoral counselors: Rebecca counselors help women suffering from the effects of an abortion; grief counselors minister to the bereaved; Stephen's counselors care for people with a variety of pastoral problems

Nature of Pastoral Counseling

Pastoral counseling is not the same as psychological counseling or a modified type of psychotherapy but a distinctly different process whose goals differ from psychological counseling and psychotherapy. The function of pastoral counselors is to help people of faith maintain and grow in their faith and/or solve their problems in the light of their faith; the function of psychiatry or psychology is to help people overcome some form of mental or emotional disorder.

Occasionally, one hears a priest-counselor say: "The woman I counseled tonight was too difficult for me so I referred her to Dr. Jones, the psychiatrist." If the priest meant that he was unable to help this woman with her psychological problems because her problems were too severe, one can call into question whether the priest understands the purpose of pastoral counseling. If, on the other hand, the priest meant that the woman had such severe psychological problems that these problems hindered her benefitting from pastoral counseling, and that he therefore referred her to a psychiatrist so she could improve her mental health and subsequently be more receptive of pastoral counseling, then he has a clearer understanding of the purpose of the pastoral counseling. Also, it should be noted that people like this woman may need help with matters of faith while still in psychotherapy, so the pastoral counselor should let them know that they are welcome to return while in psychotherapy if they have a problem that is related to their faith.

The main purpose of this book is to teach pastoral counselors about the various personality disorders, and then show them how these disorders impact on the faith of people who have them. Many people with personality disorders never seek any kind of psychological help, either because they do not realize that they need help or because they are adverse to it. At the same time, they may be open to pastoral care at their parish or while they are in the hospital because they see no stigma attached to the care of their souls.

A Referral

With time and experience, most pastoral counselors are able to recognize the person who is so mentally and/or emotionally disturbed that he or she is unable to hear and act upon the advice and guidance given in pastoral counseling. They realize that further pastoral counseling with these individuals will probably be fruitless and that a referral is needed. The purpose of the referral is to relieve the inner distress of the person and, if possible, ameliorate the mental or emotional disorder, at least to some extent. Then the person can lead a happier and more productive life, and later be in the position to profit from pastoral counseling.[11]

The pastoral counselor should realize that personality disorders are not easily remedied by psychiatric or psychological treatment because these disorders are usually long-standing.[12] Most personality disorders have their origin in early childhood, so that substantially changing patterns of behavior is difficult. Moreover, some personality disorders seem to have a genetic and physiological base which cannot be altered. Sometimes, the most that one can expect from psychotherapy or psychological counseling is some change in the person's thinking, attitudes or behavior. Such changes allow affected people to live more comfortably with themselves and their world because they have more control over themselves and act in a more rational manner.

When making a referral, counselors should realize that most people will oppose the suggestion that they seek therapy or psychological counseling, simply because they do not want to admit they are so mentally or emotionally disordered that they require such help. Probably, they will insist that they can handle the matter on their own and without professional help. Some may even feel insulted when a pastoral counselor suggests that they consider seeing a psychiatrist or psychologist. Therefore, a referral should be made tactfully. Initially, it should be given in a tentative way, with the counselor first asking the person if he or she has ever thought of getting professional care, and then indicating that this type of help could be beneficial to them. If the tactful suggestion meets with considerable resistance, and it is evident that the individual needs psychiatric or psychological care, then the counselor may be a little more forceful. However, one must bear in mind that people usually get little from psychotherapy or psychological counseling when they do not want it.

Before suggesting a referral, it is good to inquire whether the person has ever had psychiatric or psychological help before, and if they have, what kind, where, and with what outcome. People who have had two or three years of psychotherapy, or have seen several therapists, usually will not benefit from added psychotherapy, unless they have had a serious relapse and need more therapy to regain their former level of stability. If the person has never had psychological or psychiatric treatment before, then the counselor should try to determine what kind of disorder the person has and recall how amenable this personality disorder is to treatment. In cases where the person seems severely disturbed and there are some physical symptoms as well, such as dizziness, insomnia, or loss of appetite and weight, it sometimes helps to suggest that the person consult with his or her family physician. If the physician then makes the referral, it will often be to a psychiatrist (also a medical doctor). Some people seem to be more inclined to follow through on their physician's recommendation than on the suggestion of a pastoral counselor.

Pastoral counselors are advised to have the names of several psychiatrists, psychologists, and marriage and family counselors with whom they have some acquaintance, at least by reputation, and to whom they can refer people who need further professional care. Often the approval of a satisfied patient or client who has seen a particular psychiatrist or psychologist is one of the best recommendations pastoral counselors can get. Other sources of recommendations are the Diocesan Family Life Bureau and the local hospitals and health care organizations.

CHAPTER 2

Personality and Personality Disorders

PERSONALITY CAN BE DEFINED IN A NUMBER OF WAYS. IN THE POPU-
lar sense, personality refers to the observable, exterior qualities
of an individual. For instance, a young woman who is vivacious and outgoing is said to have a nice personality. Taken in
this sense, personality does not take into consideration the un-
observable, interior qualities of a person.

After reviewing a number of definitions of personality,
one becomes aware of two notions common to most of the definitions, namely that 1) personality is something within the individual and distinguishes one individual from another, and 2) it
is an integrated organization of characteristics and qualities and
not a disparate constellation of many characteristics, each oper-
ating independently from the other.[1]

Therefore, we shall define personality as a unique set of
organized characteristics and qualities that are deeply etched
within the person and cannot be easily eradicated; moreover,
they pervade every facet of a person's life experience.[2] This organization of characteristics and qualities includes the mental,
emotional, social, and physical aspects of an individual and can
be seen in an individual's typical way of thinking, feeling and
acting. Examples of these characteristics or qualities are ven-
turesome, dominant, sensitive, and conscientious.

In the personality, all the characteristics and qualities function together as a unit and act as the motivating forces behind
much of an individual's activity and behavior. When, for some

reason, they cease to function as an organized unit, then the personality becomes disordered.

These characteristics and their organization are relatively stable and long-lasting but can change over a long period of time. Some characteristics the individual has in common with other people, while others are unique to the individual. However, the totality of these characteristics and the way they are organized are unique to the individual and account for the fact that no two people have exactly the same personality.

Personality Development

In writing about personality, Theodore Millon says:

In the first year of life each child displays a wide variety of behaviors. Although exhibiting a measure of consistency consonant with his or her constitutional disposition, the way in which the child responds to and copes with environment tends to be largely spontaneous, changeable, and unpredictable. These seemingly random and capricious behaviors serve an important exploratory function. The child is "trying out" a variety of behavioral alternatives for dealing with his/her environment. Over time the child begins to discern which of these actions enable him to achieve his or her desires and avoid discomforts. Endowed with certain capacities, energies, and temperaments, and through experiences with parents, siblings, and peers, the child learns to discriminate which activities are both permissible and rewarding and which are not.

Tracing this sequence over time, it can be seen that a shaping process has taken place in which the child's initial range of diverse behaviors gradually becomes narrowed, selective, and finally, crystallized into preferred ways of relating to others and coping with this world. These learned behaviors not only persist but are accentuated as a result of being repetitively reinforced by a limited social environment. Given continuity in constitutional equipment and a narrow band of experiences for learning behavior alternatives, the child acquires a pattern of traits that are deeply etched and difficult to modify. These characteristics comprise his/her personality—that is, ingrained and habitual ways of psychological functioning that emerge from the individual's entire developmental history, and which, over time, come to characterize the child's "style."[3]

Temperament

The physiological basis for personality is sometimes called temperament or constitutional disposition. Twenty-five hundred years ago, the Greek philosopher Hippocrates noted four classifications of temperament which he attributed to the humors in the human body: *choleric* (hot-tempered); *sanguine* (confident), *melancholic* (moody), and *phlegmatic* (slow to act).[4] Today research psychologists reject Hippocrates' humor theory but still see human physiology, especially the brain, as the source of temperament and many personality traits. While researchers have yet to tie specific personality traits or characteristics to definite parts of the brain, they seem to be working in this direction.

DSM-III-R treats personality under the concept of traits: "Personality traits are enduring patterns of perceiving, relating to, and thinking about the environment and oneself, and are exhibited in a wide range of important social and personal contexts."[5] Traits are features of a personality that occur again and again and tend to characterize an individual. Some typical personality traits are extroversion and introversion, gregariousness, generosity, and industriousness. The unified composite of all the personality traits in a person constitutes a major part of his or her personality. Depending upon their nature, personality traits can either help or hinder our attempts to cope with problems and everyday life situations.

Personality Disorders

A personality disorder is a type of malfunctioning within a personality. A personality is said to be disordered when a cluster of deeply-ingrained personality traits become inflexible, no longer have the capacity to function properly, and impair the individual's social and occupational activity.[6] Personality disorders are characterized by developmental defects and psychopathology within the person.

The individual with a personality disorder manifests several maladaptive personality traits, such as mistrust, extreme shyness, dramatic behavior, self-absorption, lack of concern for other people's rights and needs, impulsive behavior, aggressive or overly dependent behavior, and perfectionism. One or two or several of these traits provide the basis for each of the types of personality disorders.

Individuals with a personality disorder have inflexible, maladaptive ways of relating to other people and perceiving both their environment and themselves.[7] Because of their pathological way of relating to others, they experience trouble in their love relationships and marriages. They consistently fail to see themselves as others see them. Nor do they see their maladaptive behavior as unusual. As a consequence, they usually reject any suggestion that they seek professional help. If they do seek help, they are difficult to treat because their motivation for counseling or psychotherapy is poor.

Differentiating

Personality disorders differ from psychotic conditions inasmuch as the former do not involve delusions or hallucinations. For example, the paranoid, psychotic person may be convinced that FBI agents are hiding in the basement of his house and that he must be on guard lest they kill him in his sleep, whereas the person with a personality disorder simply does not agree with the way his employer is running the office, since it is not the way *he* would run it, and repeatedly criticizes and challenges his employer.

Personality disorders also differ from neurotic disorders. People with a personality disorder usually do not experience anxiety about their maladaptive behavior and thus do not have a complex system of defense mechanisms to cope with their inner conflicts. But neurotic people are usually aware of their problems and symptoms and see a reason for change. For example, a neurotic man with agoraphobia had recurrent bouts of fear accompanied by sweating, shortness of breath, palpitations, chest pain and muscular tension whenever he left his home and wife. As a consequence, he had to take a leave of absence from his work, but he was willing to undergo treatment in a psychiatric hospital. By contrast, a woman with a schizoid personality disorder did not like to mingle with other people, lived as a recluse, and went out of her apartment only when she had to. She was unaware of the reason why she preferred to stay by herself, other than saying she was shy. Also, she experienced no physiological symptoms and so was content to do nothing about her condition.

Making a differential diagnosis between a personality disorder and a psychotic or neurotic disorder can be difficult because, at times, their behaviors are similar. Moreover, a person can have a psychotic, a neurotic and a personality disorder—all at the same time. It also should be noted that a person can have two personality disorders at the same time; some personality disorders tend to appear in certain combinations.

Prevalence of Personality Disorders

Available studies on the prevalence of personality disorders in the general population are limited in number, but the best estimates suggest that 5-15%—or about one person in ten—of the people in the United States have some kind of a personality disorder.[8] Personality disorders range in degree from mild to very severe, with the mild forms having a minimal effect upon the way the person functions at home, work and in social life, the severe forms being very disruptive.

Signs of a disorder first appear in adolescence, becoming full-blown in the young adult, and tending to fade somewhat in later adulthood.[9] People with some kind of a mild personality disorder can usually make minimal adjustments to society and at work, but may cause considerable distress to others, especially the members of their families or their employers. Unfortunately, many of these people do not realize how much distress they cause others and look upon themselves as no different than anyone else. If they have a problem, it is not their problem but someone else's. If they seek pastoral counseling, either they have been urged to do so by another person or they have encountered an immediate difficulty that has caused them to become anxious, confused or depressed.

Types of Personality Disorders

The following personality disorders, with brief descriptions of the basic characteristics of each, are treated in this book.[10]

1) *Dependent personality*. Characterized by helpless, clinging behavior, compliance and lack of initiative, and by a search for attachments in which one can lean on others for affection and security.

2) *Passive-Aggressive*. Characterized by resenting demands and suggestions from others, procrastinating, sulking, and avoiding obligations by forgetting or deliberate inefficiency.

3) *Narcissistic*. Characterized by centering one's attention on one's self to the exclusion of others, pretentious air of superiority, exploiting others for one's own advantage, extravagant fantasizing, and careless disregard for the rights of others.

4) *Histrionic*. Characterized by rapidly-changing emotional responses, by capricious and demonstrative behavior,

by an insatiable search for approval and stimulation, and by a constant need for reassurance and immediate gratification.

5) *Schizoid.* Characterized by social passivity, minimal emotional and social needs, a general listlessness and apathy, and a marked deficiency in both a capacity for and interest in maintaining warm and empathetic human relationships.

6) *Avoidant.* Characterized by mistrust and fear of others, despite longing for their acceptance and affection, and a hypersensitivity to potential demeaning and humiliation.

7) *Antisocial.* Characterized by manipulative, exploitive, dishonest behavior, lack of guilt feelings, habitual disregard for social norms and rules, and often a criminal record.

8) *Obsessive-Compulsive.* Characterized by perfectionism, being overly-conscientious, indecisive, preoccupied with details, and unable to express affection.

9) *Paranoid.* Characterized by vigilant mistrust of others, unwarranted suspiciousness, expectancy of deception, and defensiveness against anticipated criticism.

10) *Borderline.* Characterized by rapid changes in mood, tempestuous interpersonal relationships, lack of clarity in regard to self-identity, recurring periods of simultaneous feelings of rage, love, and guilt toward others.

11) *Schizotypal.* Characterized by eccentric behavior, irrelevancies in thought patterns and communication, self-absorption, and a display of an ever-present air of anxiousness or apathy.

CHAPTER 3

Dependency Disorders

BEN IS A 30-YEAR-OLD, SINGLE, UNIVERSITY GRADUATE. THE YOUN-
gest of four children, he lives with his parents. When he came
for counseling he was unemployed and spent a large part of
the day sleeping, watching television, or enjoying his hobbies.
He was active at his local parish where he taught religious education classes to young children. He had tried to teach teenagers but was unable to maintain any semblance of discipline in
the class. He also belonged to the young people's club, and
participated in their athletic but not social activities. He had
never seriously dated since, he said, he was interested in going
to the seminary and becoming a priest.

He reported that one of the parish priests was his spiritual
director and that he consulted with him as frequently as he
could. One evening, this priest received an urgent call from Ben
who wanted to schedule an appointment as soon as possible.
Ben said he had just returned from a psychiatric hospital where
he was treated for a "nervous breakdown." When Ben's mother,
who cared for his every need and was his constant confidant,
went to visit her sister in the Midwest, Ben became extremely
anxious and depressed, and was unable to sleep at night. In addition, he lost his appetite and began to lose weight rapidly.
His father became alarmed and took him to see a psychiatrist
who recommended in-patient treatment in a small local psychiatric hospital where Ben stayed for two weeks until his mother
returned.

When Ben graduated from college, at first he was unable
to find a job but finally was hired part-time by a woman friend

of his older sister. This woman owned a small printing company and took a special interest in Ben, who assisted her with photographic and graphic art projects. As long as she closely supervised him, Ben's work was acceptable, but when she left him on his own he worked very slowly and made numerous mistakes. Eventually Ben found a full-time job with a small throw-away newspaper where he worked in the layout department. Once again, as long as his supervisor worked alongside him Ben's performance was adequate. But whenever he was left on his own, he took much longer to do a layout than any other employee; Ben seemed unable to make even small decisions without consulting his supervisor or another employee. At the end of his probation period, he was let go. He tried a couple of other jobs with newspapers but with the same results.

Ben has a dependent personality disorder which is characterized by "a pervasive pattern of dependent and submissive behavior beginning by early adulthood and present in a variety of contexts."[1] People with this disorder allow others to assume responsibility for major areas of their lives because they lack self-confidence and are unable to function independently.[2]

All people are dependent on others to some degree but individuals with this disorder are dependent to an extreme degree. They feel as though they cannot get along without the constant emotional support and reassurance of other people. If this support is suddenly taken away, they become anxious and depressed, sometimes to the point of being totally incapacitated. In their attempt to please others and thus win their approval, dependent people willingly set aside their own desires and plans rather than risk provoking the displeasure of the people upon whom they are dependent.[3]

Avoid Decisions

The dependent personality disorder is fairly common and apparently found more frequently among women than men. People with this disorder will allow others to make their most important decisions. For example, an adult dependent will typically assume a passive role and allow his or her spouse to decide where they should live, what kind of job he or she should have, and with which neighbors they should be friendly. Often, dependent individuals have never had the opportunity to gain confidence in their own ability to make decisions because most of their decisions during childhood and adolescence were made for them, usually by a parent or caretaker. Moreover, whenever they did make any decision, invariably it was scrutinized or criticized. As a consequence, they became fearful of making decisions on their own, and now prefer to have others make their decisions for them. Whenever they have to make a decision, they have the urge to discuss it at length with a trusted person or persons.

Other Characteristics

Feeling insecure and lacking self-confidence are two main characteristics of most people with this disorder. Dependents tend to denigrate themselves and their accomplishments. They downplay their own abilities and strengths, and often consider the actions and views of others as better than theirs. They will even agree with an opinion that they do not hold for fear of being rejected, or do things they detest to win the approval of another person. People with this disorder will respond "yes" to a request to do a favor when the answer should have been "no," just so they can please the other party.

Fear of Abandonment

Dependents will submit to intimidation and abuse rather than risk losing the one who gives them emotional support and reassurance. They live in fear of being abandoned, of being left to make life's decisions without assistance.[4] When they lose a family member or friend upon whom they have depended for reassurance, they can be devastated by anxiety and depression, even though they have several other people on whom they can lean. Sometimes just the thought of being abandoned by or cut off from a person who has been their chief source of affirmation can provoke enough anxiety to disrupt the life of the dependent person.

Most dependents do not like to live alone. If circumstances demand that they live alone, they are uncomfortable and arrange their lives so they are around other people as much as possible. Sometimes just the realization that they can telephone or visit the person or persons upon whom they are dependent is enough to dispel their anxiety, as long as they know these people are readily available at any time. Dependents may feel a need for guidance in carrying out even the simplest tasks or making the most routine decisions, such as deciding what they should wear to an office party or at what time they should retire at night.

Again, people with this disorder are easily hurt by criticism, yet they will agree with the person giving the criticism, lest they alienate him or her. With a nurturing partner, dependent individuals can function with ease, be sociable, and display warmth and generosity; but once they feel abandoned, they are overwhelmed by paralysis and emptiness.[5] Consequently, dependents must arrange their lives so as to be in the constant presence of a trusted source of encouragement and reinforcement. "Many dependent individuals search for a single, all-powerful 'magic helper,' a partner in whom they can place their trust and depend upon to protect them from having to assume responsibilities or face the competitive struggles of life alone."[6]

Table 1. Characteristics of a Dependent Personality Disorder, as indicated by at least five of the following:
1) is unable to make everyday decisions without an excessive amount of advice or reassurance from others
2) allows others to make most of his or her important decisions, e.g. where to live, what job to take, etc.
3) agrees with people even when he or she believes they are wrong, because of fear of being rejected
4) has difficulty initiating projects or doing things on his or her own
5) volunteers to do things that are unpleasant or demeaning to get other people to like him or her
6) feels uncomfortable or helpless when alone, or goes to great lengths to avoid being alone
7) feels devastated or helpless when close relationships end
8) is frequently preoccupied with fears of abandonment
9) is easily hurt by criticism or disapproval
From the Diagnostic and Statistical Manual of Mental Disorders, 3rd Edition Revised (DSM-III-R) American Psychiatric Association

Religion

One of the major ways religious belief and practice impact on dependent people is through their relationship with church personnel. Often dependent people look to priests or ministers as being unusually gifted. As a result, they tend to seek out these people when they feel in need of advice. They take pride in any friendship with a priest, minister or sister, even when the latter has managed to keep the dependent person at bay. It is as if the dependent person is in some way a better person because of the association.

Dependent people tend to look upon God as the Great Provider and Rescuer who will take care of their every need. But they depend on God in an unhealthy way. When God fails to answer their prayers, dependent people immediately begin to fear that they are being abandoned. Just as they depend upon other people to do for them, so they also depend upon God to do what they expect of Him when they pray. If their prayers go unanswered, they fear that God has turned His back on them and they begin to waiver in their faith.

Pastoral Care of Dependency Disorder

In dealing with people who have a dependency disorder, pastoral counselors face the dilemma of how to direct and guide these people without their becoming overly-dependent on them. In keeping with their disorder, often dependents do not seek counseling on their own but rather at the suggestion of someone upon whom they have depended for a considerable length of time. If the pastoral counselor shows a special interest in the dependent person, then the dependent person latches onto him or her and begins to seek frequent guidance and advice. Moreover, if the pastoral counselor accedes to the dependent person's desire for guidance and advice and does not urge the dependent person to make decisions on his or her own, the dependent person soon has another individual caught in the web of dependency.

Frequently dependents look upon the pastoral counselor as an expert in the field of religion who will tell them what they should do and how they should live the Christian life, as well as how to resolve all their personal problems. In some cases, if the counselor accedes to these expectations, the dependent person may profit from the guidance. However, at the same time he or she will simply be developing another unhealthy relationship and eventually become even more deeply enmeshed in the dependency disorder.

Because most dependent people are so anxious to please and so fearful of abandonment, they are apt to praise the counselor profusely and tell him or her how helpful they have been. Consequently, the counselor should understand why the person offers the praise and not take it too literally. Moreover, some dependents will externally agree with the counselor when, in fact, they do not agree at all. One of the major drawbacks in giving advice to dependents is their tendency to say they accept advice, when in fact they do not. Throughout the session the counselor may hear such phrases as "You are right on" or "You give such good advice." As a consequence, the counselor may think he or she is having a greater impact on the person than has actually occurred.

Because people with this disorder seem so ready and eager to cooperate with anything the counselor proposes, there is a tendency for counselors to become overly optimistic about the outcome of counseling and to see their counseling as having gone very well. They may even think that the problem which brought the person to counseling has been solved, whereas often the truth is the dependent person has not only made little progress but has actually sunk deeper into his or her need to be dependent on others.

To help a dependent person, the counselor needs to take the stance of a friend and to avoid being authoritarian, because being authoritarian tends to foster further dependency.[10] Most of all, the counselor needs to impress upon the dependent person that counseling is a joint effort, with the counselee doing much of the work and the counselor assisting the counselee. The pastoral counselor can best help the dependent counselee by using the Socratic method of eliciting information through questioning and asking the counselee to evaluate this information, and then insisting that the counselee decide for himself or herself what is best.

Pitfalls

Sometimes there is a tendency among pastoral counselors to want to rescue the dependent person who seems so helpless in the face of seemingly insurmountable difficulties, especially if the dependent person is a woman and the counselor a man.[8] If the counselor yields to the temptation, he only strengthens the bond of dependency and runs the risk of a romantic involvement. Dependent, helpless women can activate in a man feelings of pity and sympathy, and thus render the male counselor more vulnerable to falling in love with the counselee. A willingness on the part of the male counselor to make decisions for the woman counselee and take over her life also can generate reciprocal romantic feelings in the woman counselee.[9]

Falling in Love

If the counselor finds himself entertaining romantic fantasies about the counselee and wanting to be with her as often as possible, the counselor is treading on thin ice and needs to discuss his situation with a spiritual director or fellow counselor. It is highly unlikely in this condition that he will be able to maintain the objectivity needed to be an effective pastoral counselor for this woman.

Impatience

An opposite tendency is to become impatient with the frequent demands of the dependent person, once the bond of dependency has been established, and to try to extricate oneself from this relationship. Once dependent people know that the counselor will cater to their need to depend excessively on him or her, they have a way of bringing seemingly insignificant matters to the counseling session and pleading with the counselor to tell them what they should do. They repeatedly ask for answers to questions which the counselor knows the counselee can answer for himself or herself, and sometimes better than the counselor. One woman wanted her pastoral counselor to make a number of decisions in regard to her tax returns, even though she had a tax consultant, and, moreover, knew more about the matter as a retired businesswoman than the priest who was counseling her.

Setting Limits

One of the best ways to guard against forming a bond of over-dependency is to set limits on the number of times you are willing to see the person and stick to these limits.[10] If you see the beginnings of excessive dependency, then a session only once a month is in order rather than more frequently. Telephone conversations should be discouraged and brief, and only when necessary. The counselor should remember that once the bond of dependency forms, it is very difficult to break it, short of ceasing all contact with the dependent person.

Referral and Treatment

People with this disorder seldom seek psychological treatment, unless urged by a person upon whom they are dependent. They themselves usually do not recognize their condition as unusual and so see no reason to do anything about it. If someone points out to them that they are overly-dependent, they typically deny it, or, if they admit their dependency, they think they can lessen it without outside help. It is only when they are abandoned or think they are abandoned by someone on whom they greatly depend that their personality disorder becomes a problem, and then they are open to treatment only because of their disturbing emotional state.

Severe anxiety and depression can make the dependent's life so miserable that he or she will seek professional help, but only after trying to come to terms with this emotional distress on his or her own. It is usually at the prompting of a trusted relative, friend, or a pastoral counselor that the dependent person will consult with a psychiatrist or psychologist.

When dependents lose the primary one on whom they have depended, e.g., through a falling out or death, or by simply imagining that they have been abandoned, they tend to become depressed and wonder whether they can continue life without the emotional support of this person who played such a central role in their life. As the depression deepens and the anxiety increases, dependent people begin to think they are having a mental breakdown, which, in turn, increases the feelings of anxiety and depression. They begin to have anxiety about their having anxiety and fall into even greater distress. At this point, the dependent has moved beyond the expertise of the pastoral counselor and needs to see a psychologist or psychiatrist.

If the dependent person is willing to accept pastoral counseling before the onset of anxiety and depression, he or she can probably be helped somewhat by a pastoral counselor. However, the counselor should bear in mind that a considerable amount of time and patience is needed to cope with this type of personality disorder. The counselor should expect slow progress and the inevitable development of some dependency on himself or herself, which will eventually have to be eliminated by gradually rather than abruptly ending the counseling process.

Passive-Aggressive Personality

Like the dependent personality disorder, the passive-aggressive personality disorder also involves a strong element of dependency. However, instead of feeling dependent or seeking opportunities to be dependent, the person with the passive-aggressive personality disorder subtly *resists* being dependent while at the same time wanting to be dependent. The following case is an example of a passive-aggressive personality disorder:

Jeff, a 20-year-old university student, came to the University Counseling Center because of his poor grades and his inability to get along with his roommate. When he was 10 years old, his mother and father were divorced. Jeff lived with his mother, who later married a man Jeff did not like. When Jeff finished high school, he left home and went to live with his father, who agreed to help finance his college education at a nearby university.

Initially, Jeff did well at the university, but after a time he began to spend too much time socializing and did poorly in some of his courses. The interview revealed that if he liked the teacher, he studied for the course and received a good grade; if he did not like the teacher, especially if the teacher was demanding, he would put off studying until the last minute, cram before examinations, and turn assignments in late. When he received a poor grade on an examination, he would discuss this with the teacher, who would usually suggest several strategies for improvement. At the time of the conference, Jeff would be enthusiastic about following the teacher's suggestions but he almost never did.

Jeff's roommate was a fastidious person who liked order and cleanliness, while Jeff was not the least concerned about the condition of their room. Each week, Jeff and his roommate would agree upon a time when they would clean up their room, but almost inevitably Jeff would have an intermural softball practice or have to go bicycling with his girlfriend, so he was unable to help. The roommate would clean the room by himself and then "get on" Jeff for not helping, whereupon Jeff would become sullen and not talk to his roommate for the rest of the day.

Characteristics

Passive-aggressive people have a tendency to resist the demands others place on them, as well as their own obligations and responsibilities, by inaction, dawdling, obstructionism, procrastinating, or "forgetting." They fluctuate between being obediently dependent and defiantly independent, and never really settle on either. Their verbal expression of compliance or agreement simply masks their noncompliance and the satisfaction they take from the frustration they cause others.[11] They are in conflict whether to adhere to the wishes of others or to take the initiative and act as they themselves want to act, such as the passive-aggressive housewife who had piles of magazines and old newspapers scattered all over the house that were in her way when she wanted to clean the house. Her husband repeatedly urged her to throw them out, but somehow she never found time to discard the magazines and old newspapers. Often, people with a passive-aggressive personality disorder do nothing but sit back and wait for the other person to take the lead. They use unconscious tactics to antagonize and frustrate other people.

Inasmuch as the passive-aggressive personality disorder is characterized by one essential trait, namely resistance to external demands, it differs from all other personality disorders, each of which is a complexus of a number of different interlocking traits. For this reason, some experts question whether this is truly a personality disorder or simply a single personality trait. Whether it is a disorder or not, the passive-aggressive response is frequently met in everyday interpersonal relationships and within the context of a pastoral counseling session. It is twice as prevalent in men as women.

Usually a passive-aggressive disorder is not severely handicapping, unless it interferes with achieving one's life goals. Frequently this disorder is accompanied by changing behavior and moods, with the person becoming restless, unstable, easily nettled, offended by trifles, sullen, impatient, and irritable. Passive-aggressives have a low tolerance for frustration and can be distraught and despondent one moment and joyful and enthusiastic the next.

Subtle Anger

Being passive-aggressive is a subtle way of masking one's anger. Passive-aggressive people are usually angry at the way life treats them. Frequently they feel that they have been trapped by life's circumstances, and that nothing ever turns out right for them. Somehow, whatever they do always seems to go wrong. They tend to place the blame on others, but are afraid to lash out in anger at the person they blame, and so they sit back and attack by way of inaction or procrastination, or by doing the exact opposite of what the other person wants.

> **Table 2. Characteristics of a Passive-Aggressive Personality Disorder, as indicated by at least five of the following:**
>
> 1) procrastinates, i.e. puts off things that need to be done so that deadlines are not met
>
> 2) becomes sulky, irritable, or argumentative when asked to do something he or she does not want to do
>
> 3) seems to work deliberately slowly or do a bad job on tasks that he or she does not want to do
>
> 4) protests, without justification, that others make unreasonable demands on him or her
>
> 5) avoids obligations by claiming to have "forgotten"
>
> 6) believes he or she is doing a much better job than others think he or she is doing
>
> 7) resents useful suggestions from others concerning how he or she could be productive
>
> 8) obstructs the efforts of others by failing to do his or her share of the work
>
> 9) unreasonably criticizes or scorns people in positions of authority
>
> From the Diagnostic and Statistical Manual of Mental Disorder, 3rd Edition, Revised. (DSM-III-R) American Psychiatric Association.

Pastoral Care for Passive-Aggressives

People with a passive-aggressive personality disorder may seek pastoral counseling for some other reason, but often neither the counselor nor the counselee realizes that the latter has a passive-aggressive disorder. Only after a period of time may the counselor detect passive-aggressive signs in the counselee's behavior. One of the ways this disorder manifests itself is by the person failing to put into action what he or she has decided to do as a result of the counseling. The passive-aggressive will agree to take certain action steps, but then will not take these steps. Usually, due to a limitation of time, the pastoral counselor is not in a position to help the person modify these patterns. But at least the counselor can make the person aware of this tendency, especially if it occurs in the context of a counseling session, and then point out other possible ways of acting, should the counselee find himself or herself in a similar situation.

CHAPTER 4

Self-Centered Disorders

THE NARCISSISTIC AND HISTRIONIC DISORDERS ARE TWO PERSONAL-
ity disorders whose primary characteristics are self-centeredness
and self-absorption. The following case is an example of a Narcissistic Personality Disorder.

June was a 31-year-old secretary who always dressed in
the latest fashion and beamed when anyone commented on her
stylish dressing. She had a cheerful, friendly disposition and
said everyone at the office loved her but the office manager,
who had it in for her and treated her meanly. Because of this
office manager, June said she was thinking of transferring to
another department. One of the office manager's main complaints was June's repeated tardiness and lack of consideration
for others. June seemed to want others to give her special attention but never thought of volunteering to help the other people
in the office when they needed help.

She came from a wealthy family and had three brothers
considerably older than herself. As the youngest child and only
girl in the family, she was doted on by her father and show-
ered with attention. He gave her everything she wanted, including a large wardrobe. At the same time, June was neglected
by her mother, who was an officer in the family business, seldom at home, and favored June's oldest brother.

For the most part, June was raised by servants who had
little else to do than care for her and a large house. Since her
brothers were away at boarding school while she was growing
up, June was alone much of the time and seemed to have no

34

childhood friends aside from a large family of older girls next door whom she occasionally visited.

When June was a teenager, the family business failed and her family had to radically change its standard of living, which June deeply resented because she could no longer have whatever she wanted and servants to wait on her.

When 20 years old, she moved away from her parents' home and went to live with another young woman in an apartment. During the next 10 years she was engaged to be married several times but broke off each engagement because she said the man did not live up to her expectations. Moreover, each of the relationships was plagued with violent arguments, usually over the man failing to give her the attention she wanted and whatever she wanted. After breaking off her last relationship with an older man whom June said she loved, she became depressed and sought counseling.

Narcissistic Behavior

The narcissistic personality disorder is characterized by extreme self-centeredness, an overvaluation of one's own importance and achievements, lack of empathy (recognizing and understanding the feelings of others), and hypersensitivity to criticism and devaluation.[1]

Initially, a person with a narcissistic personality disorder seems normal, friendly, and even unusually well-balanced. For the most part, narcissistic people seem to be cheerful, self-confident and imperturbable.[2] It is only after knowing them for awhile that one begins to notice that narcissistic individuals are very self-centered and seem almost oblivious to the needs and feelings of other people. People with this disorder love to talk about themselves and their ambitions, and are given to fantasizing about being in some high-ranking position in government, business, or the arts. An example of this kind of fantasizing can be seen in the bright law student who became depressed after failing to get excellent grades in two of his five courses. He no longer thought that he could become the Attorney General of the United States since he had received "good" grades rather than "excellent" ones in two of his courses.

Narcissistic people overestimate their talents and abilities. They see themselves as exceptionally gifted and cannot conceive of themselves as failing at anything.[3] They seem unable to tolerate any insinuation that they are less gifted than they think they are. If their talent is called into question or they fail to attain something they think they merit, such as a higher position at work, narcissists can react with anger, humiliation, and sometimes depression. At such times, they can be filled with self-pity and given to crying spells in private or having a temper tantrum.

Personal Appearance

People with a narcissistic disorder are given to vanity and, sometimes, arrogance.[4] They are particularly solicitous about their appearance and dress. Almost always their dress is impeccable and according to the latest style. They are completely "sold" on themselves and their ability to dress like the best people, even when they are not wealthy. They come to a counseling session wearing their finest clothes and are delighted when the counselor compliments them on how they are dressed.

Entitlement

Narcissistic people have an exaggerated sense of self-importance and see themselves as privileged, extra-special people and expect others to treat them accordingly.[5] They take it for granted that they will be held in high respect and admired by all they meet. Because they think they are special people, narcissists think they are entitled to special consideration. For example, a narcissist will cut into a line at a bank or ticket office and then cannot understand why others in the line get upset with him or her. If someone fails to treat them the way they think they deserve because of their special position, narcissists can become extremely angry and retreat into cold silence or fly into a rage. The following exemplifies this kind of behavior.

Mildred worked in a Weight Reducing Program along with two other women. Each of the women received a commission according to the number of clients they registered. The women agreed with their supervisor to take turns in registering the new customers as they came into the Center and applied for the Program. But Mildred would sometimes take one of the other women's turn in addition to her own turn, and then she could not understand why the other two workers became angry. Mildred thought that they should be willing to allow her to take their commission since she said she did this only once in awhile, and, besides, she needed the money to pay the rent for her expensive apartment. If one of the other women complained to the supervisor, Mildred would become incensed and treat both women in cold disdain for the rest of the day.

Criticism

Narcissists tend to persistently overevaluate their own importance and achievements. Occasionally, someone suggests to the narcissistic person that he or she is not as talented as he or she thinks and shakes the narcissist's underlying lack of self-esteem. Then, the narcissistic person becomes angry and feels humiliated. If the person offering the perceived insult is someone the narcissist considers superior to himself or herself, then the narcissist engages in overt rage. If, on the other hand, the narcissist feels superior to the person offering the perceived insult, the narcissist reacts with cold disdain and contempt. On the surface, narcissistic people are so completely satisfied with themselves that they cannot understand how anyone could help but feel the same. At a deeper level of their personality, however, their self-esteem is seriously threatened whenever other people call into question their ability or talent.

Privilege to Serve Them

Since people with this disorder see themselves as very special people, they think that other people should consider it a privilege to serve them or do for them, and not expect the narcissist to do anything for them in return.[6] When it comes to dealing with another person, reciprocity never enters the mind of the narcissistic person. This trait is exemplified by a narcissistic woman who, when asked what she expected of the man she hoped to marry, responded that he should be handsome, love her very much, and be willing to take care of her for the rest of her life. She expected him to do the cooking and get someone to take care of their children, if there were any children. She gave the impression that she considered the man who would marry her most fortunate, and that she had an obligation to contribute little to the partnership other than her physical presence.

Social Life

People with a narcissistic disorder usually have few close friends but a wide circle of admiring acquaintances. Their interpersonal relationships are superficial, fragile, and frequently disturbed.[7] When narcissists have a close relationship, the other person can never do enough, and narcissistic people always want more. Often the relationship is marked by fits of anger and explosive episodes with the narcissistic individual accusing the other person of not paying enough attention to them and their needs, and the other person becoming frustrated because he or she never seems able to meet the demands of the narcissistic person.

Lack of empathy (inability to recognize and experience how others feel) and failure to show any gratitude for what others have done for them are often the major contributors to the narcissist's inability to form stable, long-term relationships. It seldom enters the mind of a narcissistic person to consider how another feels about what he or she has said or done. Narcissists simply assume that the other feels the same as they do. Usually, narcissists are unaware of the suffering they cause others, even when the narcissist says or does hurtful things. Moreover, when another person does a narcissist a favor, the narcissist never thinks of expressing his or her gratitude. The person bestowing the favor is simply doing what is expected of him or her, and thus does not merit an expression of gratitude.

Usually individuals with this disorder are outgoing and ingratiating, as long as others praise and admire them. When others fail to provide the adulation the narcissist expects, or when they criticize some of the narcissist's actions, the narcissist is unable to understand why people treat him or her this way, and then can become abrasive, abrupt or rude.

Work and Achievement

When people with a narcissistic disorder join the work force, they expect to begin with a high-ranking job and advance rapidly. Aaron Beck says: "The goal of recognition motivates narcissists far more than the social value of the work they do, the relative contribution it may make to family security, or simply pleasure and enjoyment in the work."[8] When not as successful as they expected, narcissists are given to fantasizing about a position in which they have unlimited power and success. Narcissists are also prone to envy those who do better than they. An example is the narcissistic woman who, upon not being approved for a raise in the department store where she worked, daydreamed of herself as a Parisian fashion designer, even though she could neither speak French nor sew and had no experience whatsoever in the field of fashion design. It turned out that this woman was envious of the woman next door who made her living designing and selling expensive dresses to wealthy women.

Table 3. Characteristics of a Narcissistic Personality Disorder, as indicated by at least five of the following:
1) reacts to criticism with feelings of rage, shame, or humiliation (even if not expressed);
2) is interpersonally exploitive: takes advantage of others to achieve his or her own ends;
3) has a grandiose sense of self-importance, e.g., exaggerates achievements and talents, expects to be noticed as "special" without appropriate achievement;
4) believes that his or her problems are unique and can be understood only by other special people;
5) is preoccupied with fantasies of unlimited success, power, brilliance, beauty, or ideal love;
6) has a sense of entitlement; unreasonable expectation of especially favorable treatment, e.g., assumes that he or she does not have to wait in line when others must do so;
7) requires constant attention and admiration: e.g., keeps fishing for compliments;
8) lacks empathy: is unable to recognize and experience how others feel, e.g., annoyance and surprise when a friend who is seriously ill cancels a date;
9) is preoccupied with feelings of envy.
From the Diagnostic and Statistical Manual of Mental Disorders, 3rd Edition, Revised (DSM-III-R). American Psychiatric Association

Religion

An essential part of the Christian message is that Christians are called to love God with their whole mind, heart, and soul and their neighbor as themselves. People with a narcissistic personality disorder have a very difficult time grasping the significance of this message. From the perspective of their disorder, God exists to take care of them. They do not exist to serve God and all those whom God loves. Their image of God is that of a Kindly Giver, who hears and answers their every prayer. When God does not answer their prayers, narcissists can become disillusioned with religion or feel hurt, imagining that God has "let them down."

Because they are so preoccupied with themselves, the thought of helping other people seldom, if ever, enters their minds. Narcissists are oblivious to the needs and sufferings of others. For example, when a narcissistic woman complained to her counselor that she had nothing to do on weekends after she had broken up with her boyfriend, the counselor suggested that she might visit patients in a home for the aged or volunteer her services at a free clinic for homeless women and their children. But the woman dismissed this suggestion, saying she thought she would not enjoy dealing with such people and could see no reason for spending her time in such activities. She then wanted to know how *she* would be helped by doing some kind of volunteer service.

Usually, the only motive that has any meaning for narcissists is self-aggrandizement. It is not the value of helping others that moves narcissists to act but how they will look in the eyes of other people because of their acts of charity. If helping an elderly person who lives alone will be noticed by others, then the narcissist will probably agree to get involved. But if the "good deed" never comes to the attention of others, if it doesn't elicit praise, the narcissist will probably reject the opportunity. Or, having once gotten involved, he or she will likely discontinue the visits, once it becomes evident that no one has noticed them.

If people with this disorder volunteer for a parish service, they expect to be given a position where others will look up to them and praise them. They love to have their names in the parish bulletin or a church brochure, and they see no purpose in volunteering their services simply out of desire to serve the Church and/or its members. Usually narcissistic people are unable to be just workers; they have to be in charge where they will be looked upon by others as authority figures, and unfortunately, many often do not have the ability to be effective leaders.

Histrionic Personality Disorder

Unlike people with a narcissistic personality disorder who draw their security and self-esteem from their conviction that they are "special" people, people with a histrionic disorder are in constant need of attention and affection to bolster their limited self-esteem and self-confidence. The following is an example of a histrionic personality disorder.

Susan, a 30-year-old cocktail waitress, sought counseling after ending her relationship with her 50-year-old boyfriend. At the beginning of the session she was tearful and vaguely suicidal, but she brightened up within the session and became animated and coquettish. During the counseling sessions she was always attractively and seductively dressed, had carefully applied make-up, and crossed her legs in a revealing fashion. She related her story with dramatic inflections and seemed very concerned about the impression she was making. Although she cried frequently, her grief appeared to be without depth and mainly for effect.

On one occasion, when it was not possible to change her next appointment to accommodate her plans, she became visibly upset and suggested that the counselor really did not care about her but was simply interested in the fee he received.

Susan's history revealed that she is usually the life of the party and has no problem making friends—although she seems to lose them just as easily. Moreover, people sometimes accuse her of being selfish, immature, and unreliable, e.g., by arriving late for appointments or failing to repay borrowed money. She was competitive with and jealous of other women, believing they were catty and untrustworthy; and she was known for being particularly seductive with her friends' boyfriends.[9]

Characteristics of Histrionics

The essential features of a histrionic personality disorder are excessive emotionality, excitability, and attention-getting behavior.[10] The prevalence of the histrionic personality disorder is unknown but it is far more common among women than men.[11] People with this disorder are colorful, lively and dramatic, but their thinking is superficial and their emotions shallow. They are often creative and imaginative. They seem to have an insatiable need for appreciation and approval, and give the impression of being self-centered and immature.

At first meeting, histrionic people impress others as being outgoing, friendly, and talkative. They have a flair for the dramatic and a capacity to make others center the attention on themselves. They are demonstrative and excitable but easily bored with inactivity. They do not tolerate frustration, delay or disappointment; and they react with irrational, angry outbursts or temper tantrums when frustrated or disappointed.[12]

Attention-getting Devices

After dealing with histrionic people for awhile, it becomes evident that they have an all-consuming need to be noticed and to be given special attention. Histrionics actively seek expressions of admiration and praise from others through dramatic, attention-seeking behavior. Flamboyant dressing and the over-use of make-up are some of the ways histrionic women gain attention. For example, for her initial interview with a male counselor, a histrionic woman wore a gold pantsuit, fur stole, black boots and an outlandish hairdo. Often histrionics are entertaining and the life of the party; women behave in a charming and/or coquettish manner, and men are overly gracious and effusive in giving praise. On occasion, they are openly seductive.

Theodore Millon says:

> More than merely agreeable and friendly, they "sell" themselves by employing their talents and charm to elicit recognition and esteem. This is done by presenting an attractive front, by seductive pretensions, by a dilettante sophistication, and by a show of postures and acts to impress and amuse others. Displays and exhibitions, dramatic gestures, attractive coiffures, frivolous com-

ments, clever stories, and shocking clothes, all are designed not to "express themselves" but to draw interest, stimulation, and attention.[13]

Table 4. Characteristics of a Histrionic Personality Disorder, as indicated by at least four of the following:
1) constantly seeks or demands reassurance, approval or praise;
2) is inappropriately seductive in appearance and behavior;
3) is overly concerned with physical attractiveness;
4) expresses emotion with inappropriate exaggeration, e.g., embraces casual acquaintances with excessive ardor, uncontrollable sobbing on minor sentimental occasions, has temper tantrums;
5) is uncomfortable in situations in which he or she is not the center of attention;
6) displays rapidly shifting and shallow expression of emotions;
7) is self-centered, actions being directed toward obtaining immediate satisfaction; has no tolerance for the frustration of delayed gratification;
8) has a style of speech that is excessively impressionistic and lacking in detail.
From the Diagnostic and Statistical Manual of Mental Disorders, 3rd Edition, Revised (DSM-III-R). American Psychiatric Association.

Religion

In general, it can be said that religion plays a limited role in the life of most people with a histrionic personality disorder. Due to the superficiality of their thinking and shallow emotional life, histrionics often fail to see the importance or value of religion. If they belong to a church and participate in some of its activities, their motivation is usually social rather than religious. The social life of the church affords histrionics the opportunity to have other people take special notice of them and their unusual behavior and dress. If histrionics are active members of a parish and join a prayer group or social welfare activity, they do so not so much for their spiritual benefit as to have other people focus their attention on them. They do this by employing their talents and charm to elicit recognition and esteem and by being vivacious, colorful, and dramatic.[14] Once the members of the group begin to take the histrionic member for granted and give him or her the same attention as any other member, the histrionic loses interest and often ceases to attend the meetings. However, some are so desperate for attention that they remain in the group and make an all-out effort to gain the attention of at least some of the members. When this happens, the behavior of the histrionic can become very annoying and even disruptive.

Pastoral Counseling

In pastoral counseling, both narcissistic and histrionic people expect to receive special consideration. The former think they should get special consideration because they assume that they are the most important persons the counselor is counseling. The latter strives for special consideration on the part of others because it serves to bolster their limited self-esteem. Both are convinced that they deserve special treatment from the pastoral counselor. And if they do not receive this kind of treatment, they become annoyed and lose interest in the counseling. Accordingly, pastoral counselors should make a special effort to show people with either of these disorders that they are, indeed, interested in helping them. At the same time, the counselor needs to recognize that he or she may not be able to give narcissists and histrionics all the special consideration such people want and feel they deserve.

Focusing on Others

Since people with either of these disorders are so extremely self-centered, one of the first tasks of the pastoral counselor is to try to move the focus of the dialogue off the narcissistic or histrionic person and onto other people. Thus, the narcissist or histrionic can come to realize that, as Christians, they are called to show love and concern for other people, particularly for underprivileged and suffering people. Usually people with these two disorders are set in their ways of thinking and any change comes only with great difficulty. Consequently, the pastoral counselor should not become discouraged if the counselee reverts time and time again to talking about himself or herself.

Nothing But the Best

People with a narcissistic disorder usually want the best or highest-ranked pastoral counselor as their counselors. If there is a priest who has had psychiatric or psychological training, the narcissistic person will prefer him over other priests. If the choice is between a priest, sister, or layperson, the narcissist will rank them in that order, regardless of how competent each is. If narcissists are assigned to a lay pastoral counselor, they may simply fail to appear for their appointment.

In coming for counseling, some narcissists may repeatedly arrive 15 or 20 minutes late without giving a thought to the inconvenience this may cause for the counselor or the counselee who is to follow them. On the other hand, if they arrive 15 minutes early, they expect to begin immediately. If they are not accommodated, they show obvious signs of annoyance. If the pastoral counselor is late for his or her appointment, narcissists become annoyed and may seem to accept no excuse for the delay.

Also, some narcissistic people do not see any reason for their counseling to be restricted to a limited amount of time. They think that if the pastoral counselor were really interested in helping them, he or she would let them continue the session until they have finished, even if this requires two or three hours. They pay no attention to the fact that the counselor may have other people to see the same afternoon or evening. If they arrive late and know that they are to be followed by another counselee, they still demand the full hour or half-hour, and resent the next counselee taking what they consider their time. Consequently, in counseling people with this disorder, it is imperative that the pastoral counselor establish conditions for the counseling session from the very beginning and stress the importance of following these conditions. Once the time limit has been reached, the counselor should let the person know and then invite him or her to return at a later time to finish the discussion.

Even though narcissistic people recognize that their desire to be the only person the counselor sees is unrealistic, they still resent anyone else the counselor may advise and wish that they were the counselor's only focus. As a consequence, narcissistic people often think that the other person should be willing to wait until they have finished, no matter how much time he or she takes.

Histrionic People

Histrionic people also want to prolong appointments but for a different reason. The histrionic wants to be the center of the counselor's attention as long as he or she can. As a consequence, histrionics will gladly prolong a session for two or three hours, if allowed to do so, even though they really have little to discuss with the counselor other than talk about themselves, their own accomplishments and hopes. On the other hand, histrionics often will agree to terminate the counseling session before they have finished, if they are invited to return for another session at a later date.

Usually, histrionic people will take as much time as the counselor allows them and be very verbal during this period. Unfortunately, they often derive little benefit from pastoral counseling because they are so focused on themselves and have so little understanding of their behavior and emotional responses. In the course of one counseling session, histrionics are capable of running a gamut of emotions from ecstatic to crying in despair, not realizing that much of their emoting is simply to impress the counselor. Consequently, pastoral counselors should not take the histrionic's emotional reactions too seriously until they have established the validity of these reactions. For instance, some histrionics can cry with very little reason so as to win the sympathy of the counselor.

Since the thinking of histrionics is often superficial, they are often limited in their ability to think through a problem and come to a solution.[15] If the histrionic person comes with a problem that needs to be solved, he or she will often need the counselor to structure the procedure so that the problem can be solved. The counselor may need to go through the procedure step by step, and sometimes repeatedly, before the histrionic understands it.

Referral

Hysteria and narcissism were among the psychological problems first studied and treated by Sigmund Freud. At the time, these were considered psychoneurotic disturbances.[16] From the studies of Freud and later psychoanalysts have come the DSM-III-R classifications of narcissistic and histrionic personality disorders.

If a referral is needed for either of these disorders, it should be made to a professional person who has had some kind of training in psychoanalysis or psychoanalytic psychotherapy. This person may be either a psychiatrist, psychologist or psychiatric social worker. Since treating these disorders does not call for the use of medication, the referral need not be to a psychiatrist. Inasmuch as the goal of treatment is significant personality change, and as this usually takes two or three years, it is better to make the referral to an individual psychotherapist, preferably with considerable experience, than to a mental health clinic which favors short-term rather than long-term therapy. Research shows that neither short-term nor behavior therapies have proven effective in the treatment of either of these personality disorders.[17]

Most people who have either a narcissistic or histrionic personality disorder do not see their condition as serious enough to warrant psychological attention because they are not seriously handicapped in their social or occupational life. However, they may accept the suggestion that they seek professional help for some other emotional disturbance, such as a severe depression or their reaction to a severely stressful situation. Most people with these disorders are somewhat handicapped in their personal, social, and occupational lives but learn to live around their handicaps. For this reason, pastoral counselors may also have to accept these limitations and figure out ways of working around the handicapping symptoms of these disorders rather than make a referral to a psychiatrist or psychologist.

CHAPTER 5

Relating Disorders

In this chapter we shall consider together the schizoid and avoidant personality disorders. While the two are similar in their behavioral manifestations, they differ in the causes of these manifestations. The schizoid disorder appears to be more a matter of temperament while the avoidant is more the consequence of environmental influences. The following case exemplifies a schizoid disorder.

Joyce is a 36-year-old secretary for the president of a small business, a position she has held since graduating from college 15 years ago. She is bright, efficient, and knows every facet of the business. Each morning she greets the people who work with her, but, unless she needs to consult with one of them about business matters, that is the extent of her contact with them for the rest of the day. Her coworkers respect Joyce for her competency but consider her a silent, aloof person who keeps her personal life strictly to herself. She never attends office gatherings or parties and dislikes having to accompany her employer when he attends occasional meetings, where she is expected to take notes.

Joyce is single and lives alone in a condominium where she has virtually no contact with her neighbors. She almost never visits the members of her family; out of a sense of obligation, she sees her parents once or twice a year. Even though she is the godparent of a nephew and niece, she has not seen these children in several years and has no interest in establishing a relationship with them. On the few occasions when she does visit her family, Joyce feels ill-at-ease and awkward.

In her early 20s Joyce married, but the marriage lasted less than a year. Since then she has lived alone. She has no desire to remarry. She has a couple of people she calls her friends but they are not close friends. Occasionally Joyce will have a brief visit with an elderly woman who lives in the condominium next door. Her neighbors consider her a recluse who wants to be left alone, and they respect her wishes.

She attends Sunday Mass at a parish some distance away because she says she likes the services better there than at her own parish church. At this church she has never introduced herself to the pastor or become involved with any activities.

Joyce exemplifies a woman with a personality disorder that manifests itself primarily in the area of relationships. Her disorder is called a schizoid personality disorder, and is found more frequently in men than women. People with this kind of disorder neither desire nor enjoy close relationships, including relationships with the members of their own family.[1] When they are with other people they are never at ease and usually feel a good amount of tension, which causes them to avoid being with other people as much as possible.

They prefer to be "loners," with no close friends or confidants. They are quiet, "silent" people who rarely engage in casual conversation and limit their communication with others to strictly business matters. Frequently, while growing up they were aloof and distant from others, even from their parents and other members of their family, and had few or no playmates; as adults, they continue the same pattern. They almost always choose solitary activities over activities that involve other people because they are more comfortable being alone.

Schizoid individuals do not allow themselves to become attached to anything, lest they be hurt by the attachment's not living up to their expectation. They use the defense mechanism of withdrawal, staying by themselves as much as possible. They block out the real world and indulge in a rich fantasy life. "They seem to be living in an imaginary world in which people and situations are more gratifying than in reality."[2]

Love and Marriage

If they marry, it is usually out of convenience rather than a desire for married love and sexual experience. Their sex drive is minimal, so they have little or no interest in sexual activity. They find the very concept of love difficult to understand. A schizoid woman once said to me: "I really don't know what people are talking about when they say they love another person. I don't think I have had anything like that." Actually, many schizoids maintain that they rarely experience *any* strong emotions, and, in fact, they seldom manifest any strong feelings, either positive or negative. Because of their limited capacity to feel and express their emotions, schizoids are seriously handicapped when they try to form a friendship with another person. If they succeed in forming a relationship, it is usually superficial and more active on the part of the other person who often feels sorry for them.[3]

Incapacity for Friendship

Schizoid people seem to be wanting in the mental and emotional capacity to relate to another person and form a friendship with him or her. If they form a superficial friendship, the friendship is maintained only with great effort. Aaron Beck says: "Some interpret their interpersonal passivity as a sign of hostility and rejection; it does not represent an active disinterest but rather a fundamental incapacity to sense the moods and needs that are experienced by others, and that others normally expect will evoke thoughtful or empathetic responses."[4] Schizoids seem to be unable to experience the various emotional reactions needed to form interpersonal relationships. They seem to lack the ability to perceive how other people feel in a variety of situations. As a consequence, schizoids appear to others as dull, disinterested, and aloof. Although some schizoids wish they could be like other people and have friends, they feel that it is not worth the effort since these friendships are, in the first place, so difficult to establish, and, secondly, not very satisfying once they are established.

Occupations

Schizoid individuals are found in every walk of life. However, they tend to gravitate toward occupations that call for relating to things rather than people. Often they make good accountants, paperwork administrators, or secretaries, especially if they can be alone in performing their duties. "Typically, they remain in the background of social life, work quietly and unobtrusively at their jobs, and are unnoticed even by those with whom they have routine contact."[5]

If they are seen around a parish, it is only to attend a liturgy or, on occasion, a special service. Seldom, if ever, do they have contact with other parishioners. Typically they feel uncomfortable when another parishioner greets them in a friendly manner or initiates a conversation. By their body language schizoids let others know that they do not like anyone to touch them, much less give them a hug or embrace. The most they can tolerate is a formal handshake.

Interests

If schizoids have any interests, they are limited to things they can do alone and in seclusion, such as reading, collecting stamps or coins, wood-carving, or needle-work—and even these often do not seem to be pleasurable but rather a means of keeping busy. Schizoids are most content when they are busy with any kind of work which they consider an obligation. As a consequence, they make highly efficient workers. To the extent that there is any contentment in the schizoid's life, it comes from the sense that they are productive people. There seems to be little else that brings them any true joy or happiness.

Table 5. Characteristics of a Schizoid Personality Disorder, as indicated by at least four of the following:
1) Neither desires nor enjoys close relationships, including being part of a family
2) almost always chooses solitary activities
3) rarely, if ever, claims or appears to experience strong emotions, such as joy or anger
4) indicates little if any desire to have sexual experience with another person
5) is indifferent to either praise or criticism from others
6) has no close friends or confidants (or only one) other than first-degree relatives
7) is aloof and cold, rarely reciprocates gestures and facial expressions, such as smiles and nods
From the Diagnostic and Statistical Manual of Mental Disorders, 3rd Edition, Revised (DSM-III-R). American Psychiatric Association

Avoidant Personality Disorder

While the surface behavior of the person with an avoidant personality disorder is quite similar to that of the schizoid, the reasons for the behavior differ. Avoidants have both the capacity and the desire to relate with others, but fear being hurt by criticism or disapproval. Whereas schizoids seem to have neither the capacity nor the desire for social relations, "avoidant patients desire friendships and are bothered by criticism—two attributes not shared by schizoid patients, who are satisfied with little social involvement and are indifferent to being criticized by others."[6]

People with an avoidant personality disorder manifest a "pervasive pattern of social discomfort, fear of negative evaluation, and timidity, beginning by early adulthood and present in a variety of contexts."[7] Avoidant people are generally unwilling to enter into relationships, unless given an unusually strong guarantee of uncritical acceptance; consequently, they often have no close friends or confidants (or only one) other than first-degree relatives.[8]

The typical avoidant person believes he or she is socially inept and undesirable and will be rejected by anyone who really gets to know him or her.[9] Usually such people are to be found in occupations that demand few, if any, social contacts. Often, they will refuse any offer of advancement that calls for more frequent relating with others, even when that would mean a significant increase in status and salary.

In social situations, avoidants are afraid of saying something foolish or inappropriate because they are overly sensitive to potential rejection, humiliation, or shame. "They are distressed by their lack of ability to relate comfortably with others and suffer from low self-esteem. Depression, anxiety, and anger at oneself for failing to develop social relations are commonly present."[10]

Table 6. Characteristics of an Avoidant Personality Disorder, as indicated by at least four of the following:

1) is easily hurt by criticism or disapproval
2) has no close friends or confidants (or only one) other than first-degree relatives.
3) is unwilling to get involved with people unless certain of being liked
4) avoids social or occupational activities that involve significant interpersonal contact
5) is reticent in social situations for fear of saying something inappropriate or foolish, or being unable to answer a question
6) fears being embarrassed by blushing, crying, or showing signs of anxiety in front of other people
7) exaggerates the potential difficulties, physical dangers, or risks involved in doing something ordinary but outside his or her usual routine

From the Diagnostic and Statistical Manual of Mental Disorders, 3rd Edition, Revised (DSM-III-R) American Psychiatric Association.

Religion

Since people relate to God as they relate to other people, it should not be surprising that both schizoid and avoidant people find relating to God more difficult than most other people. Just as schizoids and avoidants are able to relate to others only with great effort, so too does relating to God demand great effort on their part. Of course, God can give special graces to anyone, regardless of his or her psychological condition, so schizoid and avoidant individuals can develop a close relationship with God. Schizoids and avoidants, however, have a more difficult time making use of God's gift of grace because of the deficiencies in their personalities.

Individuals who happen to have a schizoid personality disorder are deprived, to a considerable degree, of the emotional component of religious experience; thus, they must base their relationship with God almost entirely on an intellectual approach.[11] Often their religion is an intellectual exercise learned as children and adolescents, or perhaps at the time of their conversion as adults. Usually their faith developed almost exclusively from their reading and thinking, and not as a result of any emotional experiences. Loving God and accepting that God loves them are very difficult concepts for schizoid people to grasp precisely because the very experience of love is so foreign to them.

Schizoid people usually relate to God through structured and formal prayer, such as those recited at Mass or read from a prayer book. If they are dedicated people, their daily prayer consists of meditation, which is cognitive rather than affective. They avoid participating in group or shared prayer because they realize how limited they are in communication skills and how difficult it is for them to manifest their inner thoughts and feelings.

In contrast to the schizoid person, people with an avoidant personality disorder want to relate to others but are afraid to do so, and often take their fear into their attempt to relate to God. The avoidant is more likely to see God as all-powerful and threatening rather than as personal and loving. For the avoidant, God is someone to be feared because He demands strict adherence to all His laws and commandments and will one day punish them for errors. Due to their low self-esteem, they find it hard to accept that God loves them. Their psychological disability puts a wall between themselves and God because they simply cannot understand how God can care about them.

Pastoral Care

Both schizoids and avoidants are likely to come for pastoral counseling only after they have experienced a crisis or tragedy which has severely shaken them. Usually, they come only at the urging of someone who is aware of their mental and emotional state and their need for help. Since both types have a problem relating to others and communicating with others, the pastoral counselor should expect that both will find counseling very difficult. This means that the counselor will probably have to be quite direct in dealing with them, e.g., by giving advice and guidance rather than helping the person solve his or her own problem.

Because schizoid and avoidant people are frequently incapable of carrying on a dialogue as other people do, the counselor should expect to do most of the talking. People with these disorders seem unable to tell the counselor what is on their mind or what is the matter with them: schizoids because they are limited in communication skills and frequently have no real desire to talk with the counselor; and avoidants because they are afraid to reveal anything that might provoke disapproval or criticism. Consequently, pastoral counselors should expect that they will have to pry information out of these counselees, and even after much prying still not have a clear picture of the problem disturbing them.

Questioning

To be effective in dealing with schizoids or avoidants, the counselor must be skilled in asking questions that elicit the specific problem at issue. The schizoid does not have the communication skills needed to describe his or her problem, and the avoidant is extremely defensive and therefore wants to reveal as little about himself or herself as possible. Frequently, schizoids and avoidants answer questions with as few words as possible: "Yes," "No," "Maybe," or "I don't know." To avoid such responses, it is better to use open-ended questions which cannot be answered by a single word or a couple of words.

At the same time, since periods of silence can be very threatening, especially to the schizoid counselee, they should be avoided, even if that means talking about inconsequential things such as the weather or the latest baseball game. Often schizoids and avoidants expect the counselor to give them an exhortation or sermonette, which may be the most effective way of reaching these people under the circumstances. For example, while most people are best helped by letting them talk about a grief they feel, the schizoid or avoidant usually expects you to give him or her some advice on how to handle their grief.

Referral and Treatment

For the most part, people with a schizoid personality disorder do not seek psychiatric or psychological treatment on their own, and often do not follow up on a referral.[12] It is only when the schizoid becomes severely depressed or suicidal that he or she might seek professional help but, even then, almost always at the urging of a family member, relative, friend, or a pastoral counselor. While a schizoid's depression may be lessened by medication, the underlying personality disorder will persist. Schizoids often do poorly in psychotherapy because they find it most difficult to engage in any "talking" type of therapy, develop trust in the therapist, or consistently work at changing their behavior and thought patterns. Behavior therapy is the type of treatment most likely to bring about some change for the better, depending upon the severity of the disorder; least likely to help is psychoanalytic psychotherapy.

Avoidant Personality Disorder

The treatment of the avoidant personality disorder is more apt to be successful than treatment with the schizoid. Crucial to successful psychotherapy is the avoidant's developing trust in the therapist and a willingness to work with the therapist in overcoming his or her social fears. When the therapist and client have developed a trusting therapeutic relationship, which will happen only with great difficulty and after a considerable period of time, behavior and cognitive therapy have sometimes resulted in successful therapy.

Often a psychologist or family counselor is as well qualified as a psychiatrist to treat both the avoidant and the schizoid person. However, if a depression or high level of anxiety accompanies the disorder, then these people should be referred to a psychiatrist for the potential benefit of medication.

CHAPTER 6

The Antisocial Personality

JIM, A 31-YEAR-OLD UNEMPLOYED SALESMAN, OCCASIONALLY CAME to the rectory under the guise of seeking counsel from Father Pat, who had befriended him. But his real motive was to ask for money. His visits usually came after arguments with either his former wife or a family member who had refused to give him any more money. Jim would play the martyr role, complaining to Father Pat how insensitive and cruel his former wife or family members were. Sometimes he would make the rounds of the neighboring parishes with the same story and request for money.

Jim was personable, charming, gracious, and initially liked by all who met him. He gave the impression of being genuinely interested in the personal welfare of each person he met and was quick to flatter people, especially women. Although he had few real friends, he was popular and had many acquaintances.

Jim was an alcoholic with a long history of instability. For the last couple of years he had been unemployed and lived by his wits, usually finding an older woman who was willing to support him for a while. When he worked it was usually as a salesman. He had at least a dozen jobs in the last 10 years, jobs which he either quit because he grew tired of them or was fired from due to absenteeism or neglect.

At the age of 19 Jim married a girl his own age who did not get along with her parents and wanted to leave home. They soon had three children. Shortly after the wedding, he began drinking heavily and having affairs with other women, which continued throughout the 10 stormy years of his marriage. Jim's support of his family was so sporadic that his wife had to seek secretarial work just to keep food on the table. Three hungry children seemed to be of little concern to Jim.

When his wife could no longer tolerate Jim's infidelity and irresponsibility, she packed his clothes, threw him out of the house and filed for a divorce. From the beginning of the separation, Jim failed to contribute any money for child support, always promising that he would support his children once he got a job. When his former wife threatened to take him to court, Jim sent her a check which turned out to be worthless. Previous to this he had cashed a string of bad checks, which led to his first run-in with the law.

Jim exemplifies a person with an antisocial personality disorder. This disorder involves a persistent pattern of distorted ways of thinking, feeling and acting that causes people to engage in harmful and often violent actions without feeling guilty. The antisocial person seeks to satisfy his or her own immediate interests with little or no regard for law or social consequences.[1] The disorder is called antisocial because the person attacks society and its people.

A person with this disorder acts in an impulsive, irresponsible manner and frequently violates the rules of society. In the past, such people were called psychopaths, and later sociopaths. The term "psychopath" was abandoned because it was too broad in meaning and became pejorative. "Sociopath" is still sometimes used, but has generally given way to antisocial personality disorder, the term used in the Diagnostic and Statistical Manual III-R.

Two Types

There are two types of antisocial personalities: 1) the personable, superficially charming individual who lacks respect for the rights of other people, is sometimes referred to as a "con man," and may live on the edge of criminality; and 2) the belligerent, antagonistic person who shows little concern for the law and the rights of others, and whose kind make up a large segment of the criminal element in the country. Both types harbor a great deal of hostility; they differ in the way they handle these emotions. The belligerent antisocial person openly manifests his or her hostility by being antagonistic and uncooperative, while the personable antisocial uses charm and graciousness to mask hostility, win the admiration of the other people, and get them to do what he or she wants. Both are self-centered, seem to be devoid of guilt feelings, and spend much of their time pursuing their own self-glorification.

Demographics

The antisocial personality disorder affects 3% of American men as compared with 1% of women. Men are more prone than women to act out their disorder by committing sensational and violent crimes. The proportion of antisocial prison inmates may run as high as 75%.[2] Manifestations of this disorder in childhood distinguish the antisocial prisoner from the rest of the prison population. As children, antisocials often engaged in truancy, running away, sexual perversion, stealing, and a number of other delinquent behaviors. The disorder is most active during the person's 20s, lessens during the 30s, and may remit after the 40s.[3]

Self-aggrandizement

Antisocials are self-centered. They look upon themselves as important people and expect others to treat them as important people. Much of the time they act on impulse with little or no regard for the rights of other people, and firmly believe they are right in acting this way. They resent criticism. They need to be the center of attention and, if the spotlight is focused elsewhere, the antisocial can become jealous and despondent. While gracious antisocials spend much of their time trying to win the adulation and admiration of others by flattery and an all-out effort to be pleasing, they are often oblivious to how others really feel.[4] Empathy is not the antisocial's strong point.

Antisocial people seldom, if ever, realize how much distress they cause others by their dishonest and manipulative behavior. When an antisocial man finds himself in a situation in which he is not appreciated and complemented, he quickly abandons the project and looks for another enterprise that will bring him more praise and adulation.

Lack of Trust

Failing to trust others seems to be at the root of an antisocial personality disorder.[5] Antisocial people have never learned how to trust. Many come from dysfunctional families in which one or both parents were antisocial themselves, addicted to alcohol or drugs, or physically or emotionally abusive. As a consequence, the antisocial person is unable to trust his parents, which is later generalized to all other people.

More often than not, antisocials feel that other people are trying to use and manipulate them, just as they themselves use and manipulate other people. No matter how much a person does for them, the antisocial person is convinced that personal gain is the only motive behind what the other person has done for them. Most antisocials seem unable to comprehend how another person can do something nice for them, simply out of his or her liking for them, and not for some ulterior motive. Much less are they able to understand how people can act simply out of friendship or love. In the back of their minds is the question: "What is he or she trying to get out of me?" or "What is he or she going to get out of this?" because this is the way antisocials themselves think.

Manipulating and Lying

Antisocial people are adept at manipulating and exploiting other people, and often control others by intimidation and deception. Personable antisocials are usually poised and gracious in the way they go about these stratagems; belligerent antisocials, aggressive and threatening. Both are habitual and often extraordinarily convincing liars. Lying is a way of life for them and becomes almost automatic.

> They tell outright untruths, they distort the facts, they tell just enough misleading partial truth to allay suspicion; they confess to have lied, announce that they are going to tell the truth, and then tell another lie. They offer insincere apologies, and make promises they do not intend to keep. They conceal what they are doing by equivocation, evasiveness, vagueness, silence, minimizing, and pretending to forget. They may use aliases and elaborate false biographies. But deception for the antisocial personality is often an end in itself, a way of exercising momentary power.[6]

Playing for Sympathy

Playing on the sympathy of another person is another ploy used by the antisocial. For instance, a doctor tells an antisocial man that he has skin cancer which could become serious if left untreated but can be easily treated now. The antisocial tells his relatives and friends that he has cancer, and that it could be terminal. Using this half-truth, he gets a great deal more attention and sympathy than he would have otherwise received.

In altercations, antisocials like to appear as innocent victims. They are right; the other person is wrong. They have been treated unjustly and want you to side with them. If the antisocial man has fought with his wife, his wife is at fault. If she would just do what he wants, they would not argue. Often the root of the dispute is his wife's failure to give him the attention and praise he demands of her. If the argument becomes heated, the antisocial can become physically abusive, especially if he has a violent temper.

Borrowing Money

Because antisocials are frequently in need of money, they often appeal to family members, relatives or friends for loans. Though they assure repayment "next week," they really have no intention of repaying the debt. When the relative or friend has repeatedly lent money for which he has never been repaid, he or she finally turns on the antisocial in a fit of anger and refuses to loan him another penny. Then the antisocial cannot understand why the relative or friend is so upset and treats him so cruelly. He thinks that he does not deserve such treatment. After all, every time he asked for a loan, he needed the money, and the fact that he needed the money is the all-important thing.

If the antisocial is in business, he is often enthusiastic about a big deal he is about to swing, tries to sell an unsuspecting acquaintance on the deal, and hopes to borrow several thousand dollars with no intention of ever repaying the debt. He will blatantly lie about his intentions and see nothing wrong with his actions. For the antisocial, lying is permissible, and can even be the right thing to do, if it furthers his ambitions. The antisocial person has his own pragmatic code of morality, which can be summed up as: "Anything that furthers my ambitions or goals is right." The same action or actions may or may not be right for others but they are for him because it is very important that he get what he wants. Morality is pragmatic and based on what furthers the antisocial's purposes.

Rewards and Punishments

The actions of antisocial people are based on rewards and punishments. If an action promises to win the esteem of another or bring a significant financial gain, then it is to be pursued at all costs. If behaving in a certain manner risks a jail or prison sentence, with the odds in favor of being caught, then the antisocial does not want to get involved. However, if he thinks he can outsmart the law, then he goes for it. Antisocials seldom, if ever, learn from experience. They have been known to commit, within a few months after serving a six or seven-year sentence, the same crime that put them in prison in the first place.

Making Money

Antisocials with business acumen are capable of making a million dollars—and losing it—all within a relatively short period of time. They are impulsive and willing to take great and often foolish risks. Sometimes they win and make a fortune; more often they don't and lose what they previously made. To achieve their ends, they become adept at circumventing or even bending the law. Bright antisocials (and the majority of antisocials seem to be bright) are prone to become involved in "wildcat" investments or "shady" business ventures.

Employment

Many antisocial people are unable to keep a job for any length of time. They change jobs frequently, and may eventually end up unemployable. When this happens, they manage to find someone to support them, at least on a subsistence level. While unemployed, they often complain about not getting enough money to live on according to the standard they think they are entitled to. Usually they do not stay at a job for any length of time because that would demand some consistent effort on their part, which they are unable to give.[7] They usually quit working because they cannot tolerate the constraint of regular employment. If an antisocial person is fired, it is frequently because of absenteeism and alcoholism. If antisocials are married, more often than not they are unable to support their families, so the spouse has to work to support both the antisocial and the family. Frequently, a marriage involving an antisocial ends in divorce.

Shallow Emotions

One of the main characteristics of an antisocial personality is shallow or superficial emotional reactions.[8] Antisocial people have little depth to their emotions and have little feeling for other people. Most of them are incapable of an intimate love relationship. If an antisocial marries, it is usually not out of love but rather to have someone take care of them and satisfy their sexual needs.

Family Life

Alcoholism and drug abuse are prevalent among antisocials and often lead to spouse and/or child abuse. Often, any money an antisocial acquires goes to maintaining his addiction rather than to supporting his family. This is because he has little or no feeling for his family. Since antisocials are self-centered and concerned primarily with their own personal well-being, their families exist to take care of them, and not the other way around.[9] For example, an antisocial man expects his wife to have his dinner ready for him when he arrives home from work, even though he has repeatedly failed to come home for dinner on time or, on occasion, has not come home at all. If his dinner is not ready when he wants it, he may become enraged and physically abusive. Again, when he arrives home from work, he expects his children to drop everything and run to greet him, and then spend the rest of the evening doing what he wants. If his children fail to show him the affection and respect he expects, he becomes angry and either physically or verbally abuses them. Then he blames his wife for not raising their children correctly or turning them against him.

Antisocial Woman

The antisocial woman, married and with children, is apt to be irresponsible in caring for the children. She often leaves them unattended or depends on relatives or neighbors to care for them; she is likely to neglect their medical needs when they are sick. If she is a single woman in her 30s or 40s, she is apt to have been married before or lived with a number of men toward whom she has had little or no feeling, and then only as long as these men supported her in the style of life she expected. When she decided that the man was no longer useful, she readily abandoned him for another. Antisocial women are also prone to become involved in prostitution or running houses of prostitution. For the most part, antisocial women do not engage in violent, sensational crimes, and thus are less conspicuous in society than antisocial men.

Belligerent Antisocial

The following case illustrates a person with a belligerent antisocial personality disorder and is presented by way of contrast to the case of Jim, the personable antisocial.

A woman in her late 50s came to the parish office to seek help for her 21-year-old, youngest son, Dale, whom she described as the "black sheep" of the family, having been in trouble since he was a small boy. In elementary school, Dale was expelled from the parochial school because of insolence, truancy, and fighting. In the public school, she said he ran with the wrong crowd and became involved in drugs and, later, burglaries to finance his cocaine habit. Recently, he was involved in a shooting incident in which a bystander was killed two blocks away from the local public high school where Dale had been selling drugs. He was presently in jail awaiting trial. The woman asked the parish priest if he would visit her son and "talk some sense into his head."

The belligerent antisocial, usually a man, differs from the personable antisocial insofar as he is overly aggressive and threatening to others. Still they both have the same inner personality characteristics. Like the personable antisocial, the belligerent appears to be devoid of anxiety and guilt, even when he has committed the worst of crimes. For example, a belligerent antisocial will hire teenagers to sell drugs to junior high school children, kill one whom he suspects has become an informant, and not feel guilty about this action. He will justify what he did by saying he had to do it to protect his business.

The following are some of the serious and often violent crimes commonly committed by belligerent antisocials: assault and battery, drug trafficking, forgery, burglary, armed robbery, spouse and child abuse, rape, and murder. When questioned, the belligerent antisocial will tell you that all these crimes are morally wrong for others, but that when he commits one of these crimes it is justified on the grounds that the other person deserved it or the attainment of his ends necessitated it.

Table 7. Characteristics of an Antisocial Personality Disorder as indicated by at least four of the following:

1) is unable to sustain consistent work or academic behavior.

2) fails to conform to social norms with respect to the law and repeatedly performs antisocial acts that are grounds for arrest.

3) is irritable and aggressive as indicated by physical fights or assaults.

4) repeatedly fails to honor financial obligations.

5) fails to plan ahead and is impulsive.

6) has no regard for the truth, as indicated by lying, using aliases, and "conning" others.

7) is reckless in regard to safety.

8) lacks ability to function as a responsible parent.

9) is unable to sustain a totally monogamous relationship for any length of time.

10) lacks remorse and guilt

From the Diagnostic and Statistical Manual of Mental Disorders, 3rd Edition, Revised (DSM-III-R) American Psychiatric Association.

Religion

In general, if antisocials are religious people, their faith plays a limited role in their daily lives. Although some, it is true, are convinced Christians, they fail to practice what they believe with any regularity. Others have periods of heightened enthusiasm and involvement, but they do not sustain this over time. They usually move readily from one new movement in the Church to another.

Still others simply exploit religion for their own ends. For them, religion provides merely another avenue for gaining the esteem of others or acquiring money or power. When antisocials practice their religion or become involved in church activities, their primary motive is often to have others look upon them as being good people or outstanding benefactors of the church, a reputation which deeply gratifies the antisocial.

When personable antisocials become involved in a church project, they initially show great enthusiasm but with the passing of time this enthusiasm wanes. They spend less and less time and energy on the project until they finally abandon it altogether. Few antisocial people persevere for any length of time at a church project, unless they are constantly receiving the admiration and praise of others for the part they played in the project.

Relating to God

If antisocial individuals have any spirituality, there is little depth to it. They relate to God as they relate to people—in a superficial and pragmatic manner. Fear of being condemned to hell is the principal motivating force behind their practice of what they believe. With some antisocials this fear is strong enough to keep them from committing violent acts against another person. Their religious practice usually consists of doing what they consider the minimum to escape eternal damnation, such as attending Sunday Mass or services and occasionally turning to God in prayer. Sometimes antisocials simply use

God to fulfill their own ends. When they think that God has failed them by not giving them what they asked for, they react with anger and resentment.

Underdeveloped Conscience

Most antisocials have an underdeveloped conscience.[10] They know what is right and wrong and can discuss moral issues intelligently, but are unable to accept that moral principles apply to them. Intellectually, they can accept the Christian code of morality but they don't feel guilty when they violate this code. The meaning and significance of sin is very hard for antisocials to understand. Accomplishing their own purposes has much more meaning than sinning. For example, an antisocial young man stole an expensive leather jacket from a local clothing store. He knew this was wrong, but experienced no guilt or remorse for what he had done, since, he said, he needed the jacket to be accepted by his motorcycle club and did not have the money to buy the jacket. Moreover, he told himself that the store made a lot of money and could afford to give him the leather jacket, if it wanted to.

> Partly because his own feelings are so often shallow, fleeting, and unauthentic, the antisocial personality seems to have little sense of the anguish his actions cause (especially for his family) and almost no sense of how others see him. He seems unaware of what the most important experiences of life mean to other people. When he can no longer deny his crimes, he may present them as though they were mere amiable mischief and pranks. He is able to talk with facility about his feelings and may be very good at producing "insight" of the sort he thinks the person he is talking to wants to hear.[11]

Pastoral Counseling

People with an antisocial personality disorder will seek pastoral counseling in two instances: 1) in moments of self-dis-

gust when they can no longer stand their own selfish and turbulent lives; and 2) when they need a favor from the counselor
to attain what they want. Not infrequently, antisocials become
disgusted with themselves, with the way they are wasting their
lives. This motivates them to sincerely want to change. At such
times, the antisocial becomes despondent or even depressed,
and may seek help from a pastoral counselor. One of the
things that makes many Christian antisocials depressed is a realization of their sinfulness and a consequent fear of going to
hell because of their sins. Some antisocials are also concerned
about their future and see that they are wasting their lives and
will certainly be condemned if they continue to live as they do.
Unfortunately, many antisocial people cannot sustain the desire
to change their lives for any length of time and consequently,
they revert to their old ways of acting.

Many antisocial people prefer to think of their problems
as spiritual rather than psychological because a spiritual problem is more respectable than a psychological one. For this reason, they are willing to seek the help of a pastoral counselor
who is considered an authority in spiritual matters rather than
a psychiatrist or psychologist who is an authority in mental
disorders. To seek the help of a psychiatrist or psychologist
would be to admit to themselves that they have some kind of a
psychological disorder. It is much easier for antisocials to tell
themselves that all their difficulties are spiritual in nature and
can be cured by a good confession.

Antisocial people usually are unable to sustain their motivation for coming for pastoral counseling, and often stop coming after the first or second session. Even when they themselves
have asked to return for another session, they frequently fail to
show up for the appointment. Sometimes, antisocials approach
the initial counseling session with the conviction that the counselor will solve all their problems by offering some words of
advice and make few or no demands of them.

Focusing

Because of the antisocial's tendency to lose interest and drop out of almost any involvement, it is imperative that the counseling focus on just one immediate piece of behavior that is important to the antisocial person and needs to be changed; e.g., their behavior which has prompted the threat of being fired or a turbulent relationship with a spouse who now plans to leave. Then the counselee with the help of the counselor needs to plan strategies to cope with the immediate situation. If antisocials can see that the counseling session is going somewhere, and there is some hope of making progress, they are more likely to implement what was decided in the counseling session and stay with the counseling.

Since antisocials understand the world primarily in terms of what the world does for them, the counselor should constantly emphasize what the counselee is going to get out of any change in behavior they make. In addition, the pastoral counselor should stay away from trying to discover the cause or causes of the antisocial's abnormal behavior; antisocial individuals will only use these discoveries as an excuse not to change and blame deviant behavior on these discoveries.

Antisocial people bring into the counseling interview the same "conning" techniques they use in everyday life. For one, they are prone to say whatever they think the counselor wants to hear rather than what they really think.[12] Another technique is to talk about generalities, and not specifics. The antisocial counselee needs to hear basic moral principles dealing with specific wrongdoing. General discussions of contemporary moral theology should be avoided, especially when the antisocial appears to be knowledgeable in the area. He or she may use such knowledge of theology to impress the counselor and thereby divert the dialogue away from what he or she should face.

Personal Ambitions

Another reason why the antisocial may come for pastoral care is to further a personal goal. He or she may ask the pastoral counselor for a favor, such as for financial assistance. Often antisocials do not reveal their real reason for coming until close to the end of the counseling sessions. All that they said before this time was meant to set up the counselor to grant the favor the antisocial asks. More often than not, the antisocial person has no intention of seeking guidance or counseling but invents a pseudoproblem to render the counselor sympathetic. Then, at the appropriate moment, he or she presents the real reason for coming. Cooperating with such requested favors does little more than foster his or her manipulatory behavior.

Counseling the Belligerent Antisocial

The belligerent antisocial rarely seeks pastoral counseling, and then usually at the request of a judge or civil authority so as to avoid imprisonment, be released from prison, or put on probation. Under such circumstances the belligerent antisocial is often antagonistic and uncooperative. If he or she does cooperate, it will likely be in the manner of conning the counsellor, with the sole objective being to fulfill the obligation imposed by the court. At the same time, if counseling is to be the least bit successful, the counselor must gain the trust of the counselee, which can be done only after a number of sessions. The pastoral counselor needs to show that he or she is on the counselee's side and has a genuine desire to help the counselee.

What Stance to Take?

In dealing with the person who has an antisocial personality disorder, pastoral counselors often find themselves between the devil and the deep blue sea. On one hand, a show of empathy and kindness can be interpreted by the antisocial as a sign of weakness or an attempt to manipulate him or her; on the other hand, a direct, more authoritarian approach can threaten the antisocial and may scare him or her away. Research, however, shows that taking a strong, no-nonsense approach, such as a good parent might take with a child who is in trouble, is more apt to succeed than an empathetic, non-directive approach.[13]

If the counselor presents himself or herself as a self-confident expert, without being judgmental or moralizing, antisocials will look upon him or her as a strong person. Rather than tell the antisocial what he should or should not do, it is more beneficial to help the antisocial person consider the benefits to be derived from other ways of acting. It is also helpful to get antisocials to see how their previous actions have caused others to react adversely towards them, thus contributing to the problem in which they now find themselves. By all means, the pastoral counselor should avoid any confrontation that is likely to alienate the antisocial: for instance, getting into an argument over whether what the antisocial said is true or not or what he or she did is right or wrong.

Counselor's Emotional Reaction

In dealing with people with an antisocial personality disorder, counselors need to be aware of their own emotional reactions. The personable antisocial is frequently a very likeable person who initially evokes a strong positive response. At times, the counselor's strong liking for a counselee may keep the counselor from confronting this person with a painful truth about himself, hesitant to displease the counselee. On the other hand, due to his antagonistic, uncooperative behavior, the belligerent antisocial is usually not a likeable person. The angry, "chip-on-the-shoulder" antisocial who has been referred to the pastoral counselor contrary to his wishes, who refuses to talk or concocts a story to throw the counselor off the track, can be one of the most frustrating individuals a counselor encounters. Anger begets anger, so it is not surprising that some counselors become angry when faced with a belligerent antisocial person.

Frequently the only approach that gives any promise of success is to try to control manifesting one's anger by attempting to think of some of the positive qualities of the person's personality and trying to find something the belligerent person is willing to talk about, even though it may have nothing to do with the counselee's problem. It at least provides a more friendly atmosphere and the hope of eventually building a better relationship.

Pastoral counselors who want to work with antisocials need to have a sufficiently high level of self-confidence to accept angry, caustic remarks without taking them personally. They need to be calm and not quick to go on the defensive. A sense of humor certainly helps in dealing with antisocials. In addition, counselors should be reliable, consistent, and objective, and at the same time willing to admit their own shortcomings and mistakes. Above all, pastoral counselors need a world of patience, since any progress with an antisocial is unusually slow. Research shows that the personal qualities of the counselor are the best indicators of success in dealing with a belligerent antisocial.[15] Some counselors are suited for dealing with antisocial people, while others are not.

Referral and Treatment

Treatment of people with an antisocial personality disorder includes psychoanalytic psychotherapy, behavior and cognitive therapy, group therapy and support groups, pharmacological and electroconvulsive therapy, with none of these being the treatment of choice.[15] All in all, the prognosis for a cure, or even a partial cure, is poor. Most antisocials think they are normal and not in need of treatment, so they will not cooperate with treatment. For the most part, antisocials consider any recommendation by a pastoral counselor for psychological help demeaning. They are apt to ignore the recommendation, even though they assure the counselor that they intend to follow through on the referral. If a recommendation is made, it is often better to recommend a clinic or mental health agency where group therapy or support groups are more readily available. Research shows that antisocials respond more favorably to group therapy and support groups where the majority of the other members of the group are also antisocials than they do to an individual therapist or counselor.[16] The one exception is the therapist or counselor who has extensive experience in treating people with an antisocial personality disorder and has the reputation of being especially successful in this specialized type of psychotherapy.

CHAPTER 7

Obsessive-Compulsive Personality

TED, AN ACCOUNTANT AND FATHER OF TWO SONS, CAME TO CONsult his pastor about a marital problem. A couple of years ago Ted's wife had left him, saying she could no longer stand his angry tirades and his constantly berating her. Ted thought her accusations were exaggerated all out of proportion.

Before the breakup of the marriage, Ted had taken over most of his wife's household chores because she never did them to his satisfaction. On weekends, he cleaned the whole house, even though his wife had cleaned the house a couple of days before. He did the shopping because he said his wife was too extravagant, and he supervised the chores he assigned to his two sons.

In dealing with his sons, he was excessively strict. He expected too much of them in view of their being 10 and 12 years old, and never seemed satisfied with anything they did. He readily criticized, but seldom showed them any affection or complimented them. Much of the time, Ted seemed angry and had frequent explosions of anger over something either his wife or sons did.

As an accountant in a small firm, he was reserved and distant, but respected for his organizational skills and ability to handle problems. At the same time, he was known as a man with a short fuse, who was highly critical and demanding of his colleagues, especially when they fell short of his expectations. He felt that many in the accounting firm were incompetent and never should have been hired. He had no interests other than his work, his home, and the baseball teams his two sons played on. Work was his life, and he could not understand why people had to take time for a vacation or recreation.

Ted exemplifies a person with a mild obsessive-compulsive personality disorder. He was able to perform adequately at home, work, and socially but only amidst emotional upheaval within himself and those with whom he had to deal. The essential features of an obsessive-compulsive personality disorder are repeated obsessions and compulsions that interfere with an individual's functioning. An obsessive-compulsive personality disorder is characterized by a pervasive pattern of perfectionism and inflexibility, preoccupation with details, rules and regulations, excessive devotion to duty, and unreasonable insistence that others live up to his or her excessively high standards.[1]

Obsessions

The term "obsession" describes the experience of an individual who is preoccupied with intrusive and persistent thoughts, words, mental images or impulses which the person recognizes as being foolish and irrational but cannot dispel.[2] These thoughts, words or images come into the person's consciousness, and he or she is unable to suppress them, even with great effort. An example of an obsession can be found in the woman who is unable to rid herself of the thought that there are deadly germs on the surface of everything she touches and is afraid of hurting other people by spreading these germs. As a consequence, she feels compelled to wash her hands many times during the day, so as not to contaminate other people.

Obsessions usually involve doubts, hesitation, fears of contamination or of one's own aggressive impulses. A true obsession must have the following characteristics: 1) the thought, image, or impulse must be persistent, preoccupying and unwanted; 2) it must be recognized at some point by the person as being senseless and irrelevant, although he or she may become habituated and no longer see the thought or impulse as so bizarre; and 3) the experience must be actively resisted by the person as an undesirable intrusion into consciousness.[3]

Obsessions come into the minds of people in spite of their resistance and contrary to what they will. People with obsessions are usually unable to suppress them, even though they recognize them as manifestations of abnormal behavior. Fighting the obsession affords no gratification but rather increases anxiety and makes the person aware of how little control he or she has over them.[4] Sometimes, a prolonged struggle against the obsessions leads to the feeling that the situation is hopeless and nothing can be done to help the person, which, in turn, leads to depression.

Some obsessive thoughts can be terrifying, such as those of the mother who had a persistent urge to dismember her newborn daughter with a butcher knife. Other obsessions are humiliating and abhorrent, as in the case of the young woman plagued with fantasies of her father and herself undressing each other and engaging in a sexual embrace. Still others are confounding and exhausting, such as the university professor who feels driven to examine complex theological or philosophical questions, going over and over the pros and cons of each issue and never coming to any conclusion, and all the time seemingly unable to stop himself from engaging in this fruitless exercise.

Compulsions

Obsessions frequently lead to compulsions. Obsessions refer to mental activity, while compulsions refer to repetitive physical activity, such as the man who constantly feels a need to straighten picture frames or position the furniture in his home or the woman who washes the walls of her bathroom several times a day. Compulsions are repetitive behaviors that are performed in response to an obsession, according to certain rules, or in a stereotypical fashion. Usually they neutralize or prevent discomfort caused by persistent and annoying obsessions.[5]

Like obsessions, compulsions are unwanted and not willed. They are looked upon as senseless, but the person feels compelled to do the action. Often the more the individual fights the urge, the more compelling it becomes. Compulsive activity takes the form of counting, checking, ordering, hoarding, washing or performing a series of complicated movements that must be done in precisely the same sequence. An example of counting is found in the girl who feels she must count the number of cracks in the sidewalk on her way to school. An instance of checking is seen in the woman who has to get up several times during the night to see if she extinguished the burners on her stove and locked all the doors. Hoarding is exemplified by the man whose house is filled with piles of old magazines or newspapers until there is hardly any living space left.

Compulsive Sexual Activity

Sexual behavior seems particularly prone to compulsivity. In sexual activity compulsions take any number of forms, with perhaps the most prevalent being compulsive masturbation. Other forms of sexual activity that can become compulsive are the urge to look at pornographic literature, engage in voyeurism or exhibitionism, or engage in repeated indiscriminate intercourse. An example of compulsive sexual activity is the gay man who picked up three male prostitutes successively in the course of a single evening, had sexual contact with each of them without taking any precautions, and all the time was aware of the great risk he was taking of contracting AIDS. The main characteristics of compulsive sexuality are a driving inner urge to engage in some kind of sexual activity and a seeming loss of control. These are often followed by overwhelming feelings of guilt.

Personality Characteristics

People with an obsessive-compulsive personality disorder manifest a number of characteristic ways of thinking, feeling, and acting. First of all, they are orderly, methodical, and systematic, and expect others to act in a similar way. Any sign of disorder, either in themselves or another person, is distressing.[6] In their daily lives, they are prone to follow a rigid schedule from which they seldom deviate, and then only with great reluctance. In their thinking, they are logical, systematic and analytic, though they sometimes begin with faulty assumptions to which they may cling with dogged tenacity. An example is the man who held the premise that any lie that could in any way hurt another person is a serious sin; as a consequence, he could not have his wife tell salespeople that he was not at home, thinking it a serious sin to cheat the person out of a possible sale.

Perfectionism

Most obsessive-compulsives are perfectionists. They set unrealistic standards for themselves and expect others to follow these same standards.[7] They are dissatisfied with anything less than perfect, and if they judge their undertakings as less than perfect, they feel like they have failed. For fear of not living up to their excessively high standards, many obsessive-compulsives begin an undertaking with great anxiety and trepidation. As a consequence, they frequently put off assignments to the last minute; often, they never complete the assignment because they are not satisfied with what they have done.

Intellectually, obsessive-compulsives can accept that no human being can do everything perfectly but, affectively, they feel an inner urge to be perfect in all that they do. For example, the obsessive-compulsive college coed put off an essay assignment until the night before it was due and then stayed up into the early hours of the morning, writing and rewriting the essay. Not satisfied with any version, but out of desperation, she finally turned in something she considered mediocre at best. Later, when the teacher complimented her paper, she could not understand the praise. In her mind the paper was deserving of a far lower grade than the one she received. Then she rationalized that the only reason she received the high grade was the teacher's liking for her and her reputation as a superior student.

Putting off Decisions

Perfectionism may also lead to putting off decisions that need to be made, since the perfectionist has to be absolutely certain of making the correct decision.[8] Often perfectionists are not able to make as good a decision as they would like, and so they delay making the decision as long as they can, hoping that somehow they will not have to make it. In addition, many perfectionists have an inordinate fear of making a mistake, so rather than risk making a mistake, they ask for more time to weigh the matter and ultimately may never come to a decision.

Obsessive-Compulsives and Control

Obsessive compulsives have a strong need to keep their lives under tight control and to control other people.[9] If they see themselves out of control or losing control to another person, they become very anxious. When events happen over which they have little or no control, such as losing a job because the company where they worked went out of business, obsessive-compulsives can blame themselves for the closing of the business and overreact by becoming so depressed and incapacitated that they are unable to go out and look for another job.

While being counselled, obsessive-compulsives sometimes try to control the counseling session by keeping the dialogue on an intellectual level and veering away from looking at their own feelings or emotional reactions. One way they control the counseling session is by proposing hypothetical situations that may happen sometime in the future, and then asking for advice on how they should act in these situations. By using this ploy, obsessive-compulsives keep the discussion on an intellectual and theoretical level where they feel much more comfortable than dealing with their emotions and feelings.

Table 8. Characteristics of an Obsessive-Compulsive Personality Disorder, as indicated by at least five of the following:
1) perfectionism that interferes with task completion, e.g. inability to complete a project because their own overly strict standards are not met
2) preoccupation with details, rules, lists, order, organization, or schedules to the extent that the major point of activity is lost
3) unreasonable insistence that others submit to exactly his or her way of doing things, or unreasonable reluctance to allow others to do things because of the conviction that they will not do them correctly
4) excessive devotion to work and productivity to the exclusion of leisure activity and friendships
5) indecisiveness: decision-making is either avoided, postponed, or protracted
6) overconscientiousness, scrupulousness, and inflexibility about matters of morality, ethics, or values
7) restricted expression of affection
8) lack of generosity in giving time, money, or gifts when no personal gain is likely to result
9) inability to discard worn-out or worthless objects, even when they have no sentimental value.
From the Diagnostic and Statistical Manual of Mental Disorders, 3rd Edition, Revised (DSM-III-R) American Psychiatric Association.

Scrupulosity

If an individual is a religious person, scrupulosity is another form of obsessive-compulsive behavior that is apt to be encountered by pastoral counselors. The main characteristics of scrupulosity are an obsessive fear of committing a serious sin and a striving for perfection in making moral judgments about a sin. The following is an example of a severely scrupulous man.

Milt, a 30-year-old veterinarian, regularly attended the 8 AM Sunday Mass at his parish church. More often than not he came late because he was delayed by a rigid set of procedures he felt compelled to follow while showering and dressing. When taking his morning shower, Milt had to wash himself in a definite sequence; if he was unsure that he had followed the sequence exactly, he would begin the whole process all over again. While dressing, each piece of clothing had to be put on in a particular order. Because of his need to follow this routine exactly, Milt was frequently late for Mass.

After Mass, he usually collared one of the priests and asked whether he had committed a mortal sin by being late and driving too fast to get there. Although the priest assured him that he had not committed a mortal sin, Milt never seemed satisfied and asked the same question again, each time adding more details. Then, he would propose hypothetical cases similar to his present situation in the hope that the priest might change his response. Finally, he would ask if he had sinned by spending most of the time during Mass trying to decide whether or not he had sinned by being distracted during Mass and debating whether or not he should go to communion. When told that he had not committed a serious sin, once again Milt seemed dissatisfied with the priest's answer, and frequently would telephone another priest when he returned home and go through the same routine again.

Milt's case is typical of people who are severely afflicted with scrupulosity. Scrupulous individuals have to be absolutely certain that they have not committed a serious sin that could condemn them to hell. Since they can never have the certitude they desire, scrupulous individuals agonize over many of their thoughts and actions, examining and reexamining them to see if they may have committed a serious sin. The process of examining and reexamining their thoughts and actions can go on for days, with the scrupulous person becoming more and more filled with anxiety and fear.

Going to Confession

Once scrupulous people have made their confession, often they begin to question whether they gave the priest enough detail concerning their transgressions. Worried about whether or not they forgot to mention something important, they then feel compelled to return and repeat the same matter but add more detail.

Due to an excessively high level of anxiety, some scrupulous people cannot recall what they confessed. When they leave the confession room, often they begin to question whether they omitted an important detail which could make the confession invalid. They reason that those one or two details could change the whole situation, and so, again, they feel compelled to return to the confessional to confess this added material.

Characteristics

Some of the principal behavioral characteristics of scrupulous people are as follows: 1) they attempt to follow all the prescriptions and moral codes of their religion perfectly; and if they do not, they often feel they have committed a serious sin;[10] 2) they see serious sin where there is either no sin or only venial sin, and thus live in fear of eternal damnation; 3) venial sins or sins due to human weakness are of little or no concern to them; 4) sometimes they have such a high level of anxiety that they are incapable of making a moral judgement on whether or not their behavior was sinful.[11]

The longer the scrupulous person wrestles with a moral issue, the greater the anxiety becomes and the more difficult it is for him or her to come to a decision as to whether the act or thought is serious or not. In addition to the stress that comes from experiencing an episode of scrupulosity itself, there are other stresses that exacerbate the condition of the scrupulous person, such as domestic conflict, problems at work, or a falling out with a friend. For example, after a violent argument with her husband, a woman prone to scrupulosity finally had to admit to herself that her marriage was coming to an end and that she was worried about her future and that of her children. She was then more apt to have a severe bout of scrupulosity than when her life was on an even keel.

Religion of Obsessive Compulsives

If obsessive-compulsives (whether or not they are scrupulous) are religious people, their religion tends to be a thing of the head rather than the heart. Their faith is built more on dogmas, principles, and values than on a relationship with God. Their practice of religion is usually more in the direction of structured prayer and ritual rather than a spontaneous expression of their faith. Most people with this type of personality find distressing any kind of change in the way they have traditionally practiced their religion. Some never become at ease with the new ways in prayer and ritual, and, if they must change due to the circumstances in which they find themselves, they still long for the old way of practicing their religious belief.

Many obsessive-compulsives have trouble accepting the Psalmist's words: "God is kind and merciful" (Ps. 103). Still more difficult is accepting that God loves them, particularly if they have low self-esteem. Their God is a God of justice who weighs their every thought and action down to the last detail. If they are found wanting, they expect to be punished. In short, religious obsessive-compulsives live in fear of eternal damnation, and they ceaselessly question how they stand in God's sight.

Pastoral Care

First, let us consider some principles in dealing with any type of an obsessive-compulsive disorder, and then how to deal with a particular form of this disorder, namely scrupulosity. While trying to help obsessive compulsives, pastoral counselors should keep in mind the purpose of their counseling, namely to help people live their faith more fully and/or solve their problems in the light of their faith. They should also keep in mind the typical personality characteristics of obsessive-compulsives, namely perfectionism, the need for certitude in making decisions, and a strong belief in the existence of an absolutely correct solution.[12] Most obsessive-compulsives expect the counseling session to progress in an orderly, structured fashion, and lead to a definite conclusion. While they may come with many complaints, they are not looking for an opportunity to vent their feelings or gain emotional support. They come to counseling to find the correct solution to a problem. If they do not find the solution, they often will leave disappointed and sometimes disillusioned. If, at the time, there is no solution, the person should be told this and encouraged to live with his or her situation through the help of his or her faith.

The goal of pastoral counseling should not be to change the obsessive-compulsive's pathological ways of thinking, feeling, and acting but rather to capitalize on the person's strengths and minimize his or her limitations. Obsessive-compulsives have a number of personality traits that can be put to good use. They are particularly adept at analyzing situations and making use of a problem-solving technique, but coming to grips with their feelings about situations is much more difficult for them.

Pastoral counselors need to keep in mind that obsessive-compulsives are more thinking than feeling people. Asking the individual to go through a structured process of problem-solving in which he or she looks at possible solutions and then decides on the most logical one is more apt to be successful than, say, urging the individual to get in touch with his or her feelings about a disturbing situation. However, this does not mean that the counselor should entirely neglect feelings and emotions in the counseling process.

Counseling the Scrupulous

Whether in the counseling office or the Sacrament of Reconciliation, pastoral care for the scrupulous demands an approach tailored to the needs of each scrupulous person. It also demands a special attitude on the part of the counselor. First of all, counselors need to realize that scrupulous people have a mental disorder that distorts their way of thinking, feeling and acting, and then they need to point this fact out to the scrupulous person.

Some people have overly-delicate consciences, but their condition is very different from scrupulosity and more easily dealt with. A couple of counseling sessions consisting mostly of instruction will usually clear up the doubts of people with delicate consciences. An example can be found in the 16-year-old girl who is confused about matters of sex and in doubt as to what constitutes a sin. Some clearly-stated principles and guidance will usually clear up the doubts and confusion, whereas the same information will be of little value for the scrupulous person.

Again, there are varying degrees of scrupulosity. Those with severe scrupulosity are extremely difficult to care for, while those with a lesser degree are more amenable to advice and guidance, and the hope of success is significantly greater. In dealing with scrupulous individuals, the counselor needs to determine the level of scrupulosity, what is the problem, and then decide on what approach to take.

Ground Rules

Once the scrupulous person accepts that he or she has a personality disorder, which does not happen easily, then the pastoral counselor or confessor needs to establish new ground rules, one of which is to get the person to have a regular confessor. The person should confess only to him, follow his guidance, and go to confession at restricted intervals, such as once a month.

Before scrupulous individuals go to the Sacrament of Reconciliation, they should be advised to limit their examination of conscience to five minutes, and consider only actions or thoughts that they see as certainly seriously sinful, which is an admonition scrupulous people find extremely difficult to follow because of their difficulty with certainty. When scrupulous people make their confession, they should be advised to mention only obviously serious sins, if there are any, and then to confess these in general terms and not in the great detail they feel compelled to give. When scrupulous people begin to bring up their doubts, it is helpful for them to hear: "The matter you are talking about is not a serious sin but a scruple that comes from your psychological condition." Some scrupulous people will not accept this response because they do not want to admit that they have a personality disorder. They may turn to the subterfuge of asking whether, if they were normal, their action would be a serious sin. Since the person is not normal, it is better not to give a response to this question, but simply to repeat that he or she is not normal and has a psychological problem.

Also, some scrupulous people are helped when the confessor (and also a pastoral counselor) says that he understands the matter and will take the responsibility before God for the supposed sinful action. Because of past negative experiences, going to confession can be a painful experience that provokes great anxiety, and the longer the confession, the greater the anxiety becomes. Therefore, confessors should not allow scrupulous people to confess in great detail; they should cut in and stop the enumeration of needless details.

Guilt and Anxiety

The counselor should realize that scrupulous individuals are frequently overwhelmed with anxiety and guilt: with anxiety about their future, if they were to die in their present state of soul, and by guilt over all the putative sins they feel they have committed.[13] It is this anxiety and guilt that drives them to go over and over again their past actions to try to determine if they were sinful and then go to confession to rid themselves of these supposed sins.

Some scrupulous people make the rounds of confessors and pastoral counselors in the hope of arriving at absolute certainty by accumulating several opinions or to check on the correctness of the previous advice they have received. If the second or third confessor or counselor gives a response that is different from the first, then the individual ends up more confused than before. If the confessor or pastoral counselor suspects that the person has several people he or she consults, it is good to ask the person, and then urge him or her to follow the advice of just one confessor or counselor and not make the rounds of several.

Referral

Before making a referral, pastoral counselors should be aware that research is not optimistic in regard to curing obsessive-compulsive disorders, which seems to be especially true when psychoanalytic psychotherapy is used.[14] In some instances, however, psychoanalytic psychotherapy has helped individuals live more comfortably with their disorder and feel less depressed.

In the treatment of obsessive-compulsives, behavior therapy has proven the most successful of all the therapies, where a 75% success rate is reported in treating compulsions but a much lower rate with obsessions.[15] In general, it can be said that cures are few but a lessening of obsessions and compulsions is a usual outcome, plus an ability to live more comfortably with the remaining obsessions and compulsions. Also, the depression that frequently accompanies the personality disorder may lift as a result of psychotherapy.

Quite recently, research on pharmaceutical therapy has been encouraging. However, it is not yet understood why drugs, such as antidepressants, bring about amelioration. In treating sexual compulsions, drugs typically prescribed for manic-depressive psychotics have had some success, but the reason for the amelioration is not clear.

When psychotherapy is used, the supportive relationship between the therapist and the person suffering from the disorder appears to be a dominant factor contributing to improvement. Often pastoral counselors can establish a similar relationship with a scrupulous person and thereby, in some cases, help him or her almost as much as a psychiatrist or psychologist. However, pastoral counselors should remember that obsessive-compulsives can be very demanding of their time. If the counselor thinks that the obsessive-compulsive might be helped by medication in addition to psychotherapy, then referral should be made to a psychiatrist.

Priests as Counselors

Obsessive-compulsives who suffer from scrupulosity often prefer to see a priest, especially one who is a psychiatrist or psychologist. Behind this preference is their belief that only a priest (because of his training in moral theology) can help them resolve their doubts, since they feel that priests will not treat their doubts merely as symptoms of their personality disorder. If scrupulous people are to be helped, they must come to the point where they admit they have a personality disorder which causes them to have doubts and scruples. Therefore, the first step in treatment is to get the person to admit that he or she is suffering from a psychological disorder. Sometimes, scrupulous people's insistence that they need to consult with a priest or spiritual director rather than a psychiatrist or psychologist is simply a defense against admitting that they are mentally ill.

The counselor who tries to resolve the scrupulous person's doubts, without making it clear that the doubts are but symptoms of a personality disorder, may inadvertently strengthen this defense mechanism.

CHAPTER 8

Paranoid Personality Disorder

MICHAEL, A CLERICAL WORKER IN A GOVERNMENT AGENCY, came to his pastor to complain about the associate pastor's Sunday homily, saying that it had contained communist propaganda. He was an active member of the Blue Army and recited the rosary every day. Rarely was he seen at any parish functions other than Sunday Mass, and none of the priests in the parish knew him.

Michael was married and had no children. His wife worked and seemed to have little contact with her husband. When they were together they frequently argued, usually about his wife's friendliness with her male coworkers. Michael often accused her of having affairs with several of these men, which she vehemently denied. In addition to arguing with his wife, Michael fought with his next-door neighbor. On a number of occasions he accused the neighbor of talking about him behind his back and stealing things from his garage.

Over the course of 20 years, Michael had changed jobs many times, usually because he could not get along with other workers, whom he accused of not liking him and complaining about him to the boss. He considered most of the people with whom he worked incompetent and lacking in intelligence. At the office, he usually had little to say, and appeared to be angry about something much of the time. Occasionally, he would explode over a difference he had with someone in the office and then turn on that person with vicious invectives and accusations. For several weeks following such an outbreak, he would not talk to anyone in the office.

This government worker suffers from a psychological condition called a paranoid personality disorder, a disorder more prevalent in men than women.[1] "A paranoid personality disorder is a pervasive and unwarranted tendency, beginning by early adulthood and present in a variety of contexts, to interpret the actions of people as deliberately demeaning or threatening."[2] Paranoids are suspicious, guarded, and hostile. They tend to misread the words and actions of others as threatening. Often they respond with anger to what they erroneously interpret as deception, deprecation, and betrayal. "Their readiness to perceive hidden motives and deceit precipitates innumerable social difficulties, which then confirm and reinforce their expectations."[3] Sometimes there is a legitimate reason for the paranoid feeling the way he or she does, but the paranoid exaggerates this reason beyond all proportions.

Types of Paranoia

Besides the paranoid personality disorder, more serious forms of paranoia can be found in the paranoid schizophrenic and the psychotic paranoid. The person with a paranoid personality disorder differs from the paranoid schizophrenic inasmuch as he or she is not psychotic, can think clearly, and does not have systematic delusions of grandeur or persecution. Examples are the psychotic man who thought he was Jesus Christ or the woman who was convinced that the FBI was tracking her down and would kill her if they ever found her. Many paranoid schizophrenics suffer from disorganized thinking and are frequently disoriented as to day, time, and place. Also, schizophrenics may speak in a disjointed manner that seems to have little meaning or at least is very difficult to follow, whereas the person with a paranoid personality disorder thinks clearly and is easily understood. Occasionally, a paranoid schizophrenic comes for pastoral counseling, usually in a time of crisis, but people with a paranoid personality disorder are apt to come more frequently.

People who are paranoid and psychotic but not schizophrenic usually think clearly but manifest a complex delusional system that frequently disrupts much of their life, such as the 45-year-old, single woman who went to see the pastor of a neighboring parish to complain about her own pastor whom she accused of planting in the confessional room an electronic device that could broadcast her sins to the other women in the parish. Whenever she saw two women talking together outside the church, she immediately concluded that they were talking about her and the sins she had committed. She insisted that the neighboring pastor confront her own pastor and make him stop doing this. Because this woman is psychotic, she needs to be treated in a manner quite differently from someone with a paranoid personality disorder.

Inner Experience

People with a paranoid personality disorder are suspicious and do not trust other people.[4] Frequently they feel threatened by imagined foes; they maintain a vigilant guard against an attack. They are convinced that others are going to harm them, and often feel that other people dislike them, which may sometimes be true because of the hostile way the paranoid treats others. Ever-present anger plays a dominant role in the lives of paranoid people. Frequently, views at odds with those of the paranoid person stir up a wrath which the paranoid may or may not openly display, depending upon the situation and the paranoid's level of confidence at the time.[5]

Theodore Millon, an authority in personality disorders, says: "Troubled by mounting and inescapable evidence of inadequacy and hostility, paranoids are driven to go beyond mere denial. They not only disown these personally humiliating traits but throw them back at their real or imagined accusers. They claim that it is 'they' who are stupid, malicious, and vindictive. In contrast, they are the innocent and unfortunate victims of the incompetence and malevolence of others."[6]

Lack of Compassion

Paranoids are ever on the alert to pick up signs to verify how other people feel about them. Someone might say "Good morning" with little enthusiasm and cause the paranoid person to think that this person does not like him, when the truth of the matter is the one saying "Good morning" simply does not feel well or does not feel one way or the other about the paranoid person. At the same time, the paranoid person is usually insensitive to the feelings of others. Paranoids can devastate someone with an outburst of anger, and then wonder why the other person feels so hurt and upset. As a consequence, paranoids cause a great deal of suffering to others without ever realizing it. Any negative feelings they may have after a volatile outburst come from their feeling guilty about having done something morally wrong, and not from compassion for the person they have hurt. Paranoids seem incapable of empathy; they are hard, obdurate, and usually insensitive to the feelings of other people.

People with a paranoid personality disorder are fixed in their views and usually cannot be shaken from them. Any effort to talk paranoid people out of what they hold as true is looked upon as demeaning, or as a personal attack. In an argument, paranoids consider themselves invincible. Whenever they have the upper hand, they glory in their triumph. No matter what the issue, in their minds there is simply no possibility of their being wrong. Most paranoids think of themselves as intelligent, self-reliant and independent, much of which is a cover for their unacknowledged sense of inadequacy and lack of self-esteem.[7]

Behavior

Because paranoids are constantly being hurt by imagined or falsely-perceived attacks, they are guarded and defensive people. An innocuous question, such as asking about the number of brothers and sisters in their family, can be taken as a dangerous prying into their private affairs. Paranoids are touchy individuals who are overly sensitive to the slightest hint of criticism. Much of the time their stern demeanor reflects their inner hostility. Usually they have little capacity for laughter.

Paranoids have low self-esteem. They maintain what little self-esteem they have by focusing their attention on the faults and weaknesses of others, especially on those whom they consider strong and powerful.[8] Indeed, they project their own faults and weaknesses on other people. For example, an office worker with less than average intelligence considers her supervisor stupid and wanting in managerial skills. Whenever she, the office worker, makes a mistake, she blames it on her supervisor and is very quick to point out to her coworkers any mistake the supervisor makes. When another person in the office is given a raise or a better position, the paranoid person feels unjustly treated, thinking that *she* should have been given the raise or better position instead.[9] In the end, she rationalizes that the other person got the raise by playing up to her superior, which, she claims defiantly, *she* would never lower herself to do.

Clinging to a View

Paranoids hold doggedly to what they believe. Any suggestion that there might be an alternative way of looking at an issue meets with opposition. They are fixed in their beliefs and unwilling to compromise. Capitulating or even compromising on an issue is a sign of weakness. For example, a paranoid woman maintained that bombing abortion clinics was not only legitimate but something to be encouraged, providing it was done at night when no one was in the clinic. No amount of reasoning could make this woman even question her position, let alone come to see that such activity might not only be morally wrong but ultimately even hurt the anti-abortion cause.

Harboring Resentment

Whenever paranoids get into a heated argument which ends with each party saying some derogatory things about the other, paranoid people harbor in their minds the disturbing episode for days. They rehearse time and again what they will say to this person the next time they meet. Yet, when they do meet, the paranoid person is liable to not even acknowledge the other's presence with a greeting.

People with a paranoid personality disorder are usually very critical of others but overly sensitive to any criticism of themselves. Often the shortcomings they criticize in others are the same as their own, which they will not admit. Such a reaction is called projection.[10] For instance, a paranoid man complained to his boss that a fellow employee was lazy and incompetent when the truth was he himself was lazy and not too sure of himself on the job.

Relating to Others

Generally speaking, individuals with a paranoid personality disorder are unable to form close relationships with other people. They may have a number of acquaintances but no real friends. For the most part, they are lonely, isolated people. Suspicion and lack of trust keep them from making friends, even with the members of their own family.[11] As an excuse for not making friends, they will point out real or imagined defects in the person who may have been open to a friendship. For example, a paranoid woman had a shy, reserved acquaintance who sometimes accompanied her to church services but who refused to participate in an anti-abortion demonstration for fear of being arrested. So the paranoid woman stopped all contact with her acquaintance on the grounds that she did not want such a weak person as her friend; whereas the real reason was that she did not trust the woman and thought that sooner or later the woman would talk about her behind her back.

Reaction to Paranoids

People react to the paranoid's hostility and sometimes explosive behavior in different ways. The aggressive, secure person usually becomes angry and counterattacks. This leads to a volatile exchange, but once the incident is past, it is often forgotten. By contrast, the passive, somewhat insecure person usually feels severely hurt and withdraws into silence; if the two meet later, neither speaks to the other. For the most part, the paranoid person is unable to understand the actions of either of these individuals. The secure person is simply a heartless person who is out to destroy the paranoid, while the insecure one is weak and too soft-shelled to stand up to the paranoid. In general, because paranoids are incapable of understanding how others feel or being compassionate, they have no idea how much hurt and anguish they cause other people to suffer.[12]

Table 9. Characteristics of the Paranoid Personality Disorder, as indicated by any four of the following:

1) Expects, without sufficient basis, to be exploited or harmed by others;

2) Questions, without justification, the worthiness or trustworthiness of friends or associates;

3) Reads hidden demeaning or threatening meanings into benign remarks or events, e.g., suspects that a neighbor put out trash only to annoy him;

4) Bears grudges or is unforgiving of insults or slights;

5) Is reluctant to confide in others because of unwarranted fear that the information will be used against him or her;

6) Is easily slighted and quick to react with anger or to counterattack;

7) Questions, without justification, fidelity of spouse or sexual partner.

From the Diagnostic and Statistical Manual of Mental Disorders, 3rd Edition, Revised (DSM-III-R). American Psychiatric Association

---

Paranoids and Religion

The negative personality traits of people with a paranoid personality disorder often influence the paranoid's view and practice of religion. If paranoids are religious people, their religion is usually formal and lacking in depth. For the most part, their religious practice consists of attendance at Mass or other services and pious practices. Their prayer consists of reciting memorized prayers, such as the Lord's prayer and the rosary, or reading prayers from a prayer book. Most paranoids seem incapable of spontaneous prayer; in addition, they feel threatened by shared prayer, thinking it too personal and too revealing about their own inner life.

People who are devoted to religion and have a paranoid personality disorder tend to espouse conservative causes that are related to their faith. Some paranoids become fanatic in backing a cause, trying to force their views on almost everyone they meet, and thinking that everyone should believe and act as they do. When they meet opposition, they sometimes become angry and may attack and demean anyone who does not agree with them.

Relating to God

The way we relate to God is usually quite similar to the way we relate to other people. If we are at ease in our relationships with other people, we are usually at ease in relating to God. If our relationships to people are strained and a source of tension, the odds are that our relationship with God will be the same. Paranoids are unable to get close to anyone or let anyone get close to them because everyone appears as a threat and a potential danger.[13] Similarly, they are unable to experience a closeness to God because they usually have a stereotypical image of God as the Supreme Being who judges and punishes. Usually paranoids have a more difficult time than most fulfilling the great commandment to love God and neighbor as they love themselves, and this for two reasons: 1) they often do not love themselves, even though they may give the impression that they do; and 2) they do not trust anyone, including God.

Practice of Religion

In their religious practices, paranoids tend to be traditional and given to formalism and legalism. Only with great reluctance will they give up traditional practices. They will demand strict adherence to the letter of the law. For example, paranoids can become very upset by any deviation from the established liturgical guidelines for the celebration of the Mass. On occasion, they may even report the deviant priest to Church authorities and demand that he desist from such practices in the future or be punished. Since the Second Vatican Council, church law has reduced the number of times church members are obliged to fast and abstain from eating meat during the liturgical year. Some paranoids interpret this as the Church becoming lax in its demands; they think the Church should return to the old practices in effect before the Second Vatican Council even though, in the meantime, they themselves are not the least hesitant to take advantage of the relaxed legislation.

Pastoral Counseling

Except in times of crisis or depression, people with a paranoid personality disorder rarely seek pastoral care because they do not see themselves as mentally ill. As far as they are concerned, their grievances against others are valid and accurate. It is the offending person who needs help, not they. Sometimes, however, at the insistence of a family member or when they are in great emotional turmoil, paranoids are willing to consult with a pastoral counselor, especially if the counselor is seen as a person of stature, e.g., a priest or minister. Usually their reason for seeking help is not to remedy their personality disorder but to complain about the person whom they think has mistreated them. Their approach is to ask the counselor what they should do about this person or to convince the pastoral counselor that he or she should confront the person with the paranoid's grievance.

Do's and Don'ts

In trying to help people with any type of a paranoid disorder, there are a number of factors the helper needs to keep in mind: 1) most paranoids are convinced that no one is to be trusted, including the pastoral counselor, so the counselor must constantly act in such a way as to foster trust; 2) the paranoid person needs to know that you are on his or her side. Any indication that you are sympathetic with the person against whom the paranoid has a complaint or that you see the paranoid's grievance as unfounded can cause the paranoid to think that you do not understand his or her situation, and then to terminate the counseling; 3) paranoids are extremely sensitive to any kind of criticism, so the counselor should avoid criticism as much as possible; 4) paranoids become defensive when asked questions that seem to intrude into their personal life, such as the number of children he or she has and how he or she gets along with them; 5) they tend to misinterpret what others say, taking the words as a threat where no threat was meant; 6) they are usually angry people with their anger just below the surface and ready to explode. Pastoral counselors should expect that this anger will occasionally be directed at them and not take such anger personally; 7) in arguments, paranoid individuals will seldom admit that they are mistaken. They must always have the last word. No amount of reasoning and logic will convince paranoids that their position is wrong.

Honest, Open, and Respectful

In counseling paranoids, pastoral counselors need to be honest, open, and respectful at all times, which is not easy in view of the paranoid's hostility and stubbornness.[14] It is often better to comment on how the paranoid feels rather than on the content of what he or she has said. Keeping the focus on feelings is less likely to provoke an argument and more likely to indicate to the paranoid person that the counselor is trying to understand what the paranoid is going through. For example, in responding to a complaint the paranoid is making against another person, it is better to say: "I can understand how you must feel very angry when you think people are talking about you behind your back," rather than, "Are you sure she is talking about you behind your back?"

While counseling paranoid people, it is important that pastoral counselors keep in mind the purpose of their counseling, namely, to try to help the person live a fuller life of faith or resolve a problem in accordance with the principles and values of his or her faith. Often, of course, this can be very difficult to accomplish because of the paranoid's psychological condition and shallow faith. Pastoral counselors should not assume the role of a psychotherapist by trying to change the paranoid's attitudes or way of thinking since such change calls for special skills and techniques and a considerable amount of time. Probably the best thing the counselor can do is to offer some kind of general spiritual advice and guidance, at the same time being careful not to imply criticism of the paranoid person.

Due to their personality disabilities, paranoid people can be very difficult to help. Often all that can be expected is to build on their rigorous view of religion and rigid practice of the faith. Some paranoids may be incapable of solving their problems in accordance with the teachings of the Gospel, because they are unable to forgive those whom they are convinced have hurt them unjustly. Paranoid people find it very difficult to forgive others because they are convinced that they are justified in their grievance with the other person and that the other person should be punished. Also, they find it hard to accept an apology from another person because they say it is too easy to say "I am sorry," and, anyway most people do not really mean what they say.

Referral

If the pastoral counselor is convinced that the paranoid person needs to be referred to a psychiatrist or psychologist, there are a number of factors the counselor needs to keep in mind. First of all, the paranoid will probably resent the very suggestion that he or she needs psychiatric care and is likely never to follow through on the referral. Some may more openly object to the referral and argue strongly against it. Second, if the paranoid is an older person, he or she has probably had several contacts with psychiatrists, psychologists, and other professional helpers that accomplished little or nothing, so the likelihood of further psychotherapy helping the person is minimal. Finally, even though research on psychotherapy with paranoid personality disorders is limited, what there is suggests that psychotherapy has limited value.[15] If a referral seems indicated, probably it would be best to refer the person to a psychiatrist or psychologist experienced in Cognitive and Behavioral Therapy, whose therapy would aim at changing attitudes and ways of behaving and getting the paranoid to see how his or her way of thinking and acting is having an adverse effect on others.

Many people with a paranoid personality disorder seem to make a minimal adjustment and function in their marriage and family life, work and social relationships, and on the job without ever undergoing psychotherapy for any length of time. Frequently, the few paranoids who accept the suggestion that they seek psychiatric or psychological help terminate therapy prematurely. Often, whether the person stays in therapy depends upon how successful the therapist is in establishing a positive relationship with the paranoid, which takes a considerable amount of time. In general, people with a paranoid personality disorder should be referred to a psychologist who has had extensive experience in dealing with people with this disorder.

CHAPTER 9

Borderline Personality Disorder

AMELIA WAS A PETITE, ATTRACTIVE, SINGLE WOMAN. SHE HAD JUST turned 30 years of age and was very concerned about having passed this milestone without being settled in either a career or marriage. At times, she was depressed and confused, not knowing where her life was going; at other times, she felt perky and elated, seemingly without a care in the world. In a depressed mood she called upon her pastor who, quickly recognizing Amelia's condition as beyond his expertise, referred her to a priest-psychologist he knew. Amelia's indirect reference to suicide convinced the pastor that she needed professional help.

In her junior year of high school, Amelia's mother and her alcoholic father were divorced after years of heated and sometimes violent arguing and fighting. Up to then, Amelia had been an average student, but after the divorce she began to fail in several of her courses and seemed to lose interest in life. As far back as she could remember, Amelia's father berated and belittled her whenever he was drunk but was affectionate and affirming when sober. Her mother was an immature, ineffective parent who depended upon Amelia to care for a younger brother and sister.

After graduating from high school, Amelia moved out of her home and lived with a maternal grandmother where she stayed for almost a year until her grandmother told her to look for another place to live. While living with her grandmother, she enrolled in a community college but dropped out almost immediately.

Amelia then took a series of jobs, ranging from box girl in a supermarket to waitress to secretary, each of which was usually interspersed by months of unemployment when she was just barely able to pay her bills. She did well at each job for a short period of time but then began to argue with her boss or other employees, thinking that they had it in for her. Inevitably the pattern led to her dismissal.

Whenever Amelia was out of work, she became very anxious lest she run out of money. Since she had alienated herself from the members of her family and had no close friends, she felt very much alone and could not look to anyone for emotional support or financial help. After leaving her grandmother's home, she had a number of roommates and lived in several different homes and apartments. Though she was 30 years old and 12 years out of high school, she had never had her own apartment and seemed to have no desire to live alone.

Amelia's life could best be described as an emotional roller coaster, going from intense exhilaration to the depths of depression and despair, sometimes within a matter of hours. Due to her emotional instability and angry lashing out at others, she had alienated any friends she once had. Amelia never dated a man longer than once or twice, even though she was an attractive young woman. She always found something about the man she dated which caused her to think that he would not make a good husband. Usually she suspected that he was addicted to drugs or alcohol.

Amelia typifies the person with a borderline personality disorder. Borderline is a relatively recent psychiatric category that has come into psychiatry and psychology within the past 30 years and has appeared in the *Diagnostic and Statistical Manual* within the last 10 years. Most of what we know about the borderline personality disorder has been gathered from the clinical experience of psychiatrists and psychologists.[1] Initially, the term meant being on the borderline of a psychosis. A psychosis is a condition characterized by disorganization of the thought process, severe emotional disturbance, and loss of contact with reality, along with a number of other symptoms. Many borderline personalities may manifest some psychotic symptoms when under severe stress or due to the influence of drugs or alcohol. Such symptoms appear as phobias, compulsions, and paranoia, but they are not psychotic and seldom become psychotic.[2]

Even though the category of a borderline personality disorder is relatively new, it has become one of the more frequently-diagnosed personality disorders, both in psychiatric hospitals and outpatient facilities. It occurs three times more often among women than men and presently constitutes from 2 to 4% of the population in the U.S. and approximately 15% of the psychiatric population.[3]

Definition

In psychiatry and psychology today, the term borderline personality disorder implies a pervasive behavior pattern of the following characteristics: uncertainty as to self-identity and personal values and goals, turbulent interpersonal relationships, loneliness and fear of being alone, emotional instability, inappropriate and explosive anger, impulsive and sometimes suicidal tendencies.

Borderlines are capable of rapid and radical emotional changes. They can swing from the heights of elation to fierce anger to deep sadness in a relatively short period of time, but their moods are usually short-lived.[4] During the course of a single counseling session, borderlines can be warm and tender and then suddenly angry and obnoxious. They are capable of intense love and affection for a person, but within a matter of days shrug it off, turn against that person, and show the same intensity of love for another person. At one time, they may idolize a person and some time later humiliate and demean the same person. Frequent displays of temper and irritability, bursts of intense anger and fighting are all a part of the borderline person's life.

Borderlines shift their moods without apparent reason or stimulus. As a consequence, their lives seem to be in upheaval or turmoil much of the time, seemingly happy one moment and in a painful depression the next. It is not easy for those who live with them to understand or tolerate their fluctuations in mood, which accounts for the borderline's frequently changing residences and jobs.[5] When not engulfed by some intense emotional experience, the borderline often finds his or her life boring, empty, and uninteresting.[6]

Thought Patterns

Most borderline individuals are very rigid in their thinking and have considerable difficulty coping with inconsistent and ambiguous situations, such as an employer who is moody or sometimes affirming but at other times critical. Situations or events tend to be seen as entirely positive or entirely negative, with no in-between.[7] For a borderline woman, a male friend is seen as completely trustworthy until he falls short of her expectations, after which he is looked upon as completely untrustworthy. There is no allowance for him to have a bad day or occasionally not live up to her expectations.

Impulsive

Borderline people have a problem controlling their impulses. Sometimes impulsiveness is chronic and seemingly triggered without any outside reason; at other times, it appears as a direct response to blows at self-esteem or fears of being abandoned.[8] Impulsiveness shows itself in such self-destructive behaviors as alcohol and drug abuse, compulsive spending, shoplifting, reckless driving, binge eating, gambling, financial mismanagement, and suicidal and self-mutilating behavior.

Stormy Relationships

Due to their emotional instability and a hypersensitivity to rejection and being alone, the borderline's relationship with the members of her family is frequently stormy and marked by a

recurrent cycle of confrontations, fights, separations and recon-
ciliations.[9] The same sequence is true with lovers and friends,
only more often than not there is a final severing of the relationship without any possibility of reconciliation because the
other party has taken as much as he or she can endure.

> Borderline personalities cannot tolerate being alone. Yet
> their relationships with others are intense and at the
> same time unstable, self-preoccupied, and emotionally
> shallow. They manipulate friends, family, and lovers by
> suicidal gestures, hypochondriacal complaints, mislead-
> ing messages and provocative actions. They alternately
> idealize others and denigrate them. They are intensely,
> angrily demanding, with little tact or consideration for
> others' needs and feelings; their rage alternates with a
> childish, clinging dependency.[10]

On the Job

At the beginning of employment, borderlines are personable and friendly, but as time goes on they become argumentative and difficult. Their immediate supervisors and the people
who work with them soon become annoyed by their moodiness
and failure to be cooperative. Since borderlines lack trust in
others, they tend to look for signs to validate their conviction
that most people should not be trusted. Unfortunately, by mis-
interpreting the words and actions of others they can find reasons for not trusting almost everyone they deal with.

When employed, borderlines are apt to think that their
employer or supervisor is looking for reasons to fire them.
Some borderline people go so far as to think that they are the
victims of an office-wide plot to get rid of them. Also, it should
be noted that borderline people provoke others to reject them
simply by what they say and how they act, and then by playing the role of the unjustly-treated victim. Once the borderline
builds up hostility toward another person, what had been a
positive relationship quickly turns negative. Forming intimate
or close relationships is problematic since such relationships are

threatening to the borderline and are rarely peaceful and lasting.[11]

Self-Identity, Goals, and Values

Self-identity implies an understanding of who one is as an individual; a part of self-identity is the individual's gender and personal goals and values. Borderlines are often confused in regard to their gender orientation, the goals they should pursue, and the values they should follow.[12] Some borderline people are not settled in their sexual orientation and question whether they are masculine or feminine.

Often they have not formulated a set of values that determine how they should act and what they should consider important in their lives. Frequently they are adrift, questioning where their life is going, and seem to have no long-term goals. This may explain in part why they seldom find an occupation they want to make their life's work. The absence of long term goals, along with emotional instability, may also explain why many borderline people do poorly in school and often fail to finish their education. Borderlines have been poetically described as people adrift in a sea marked by one storm after another, with the sun breaking through only occasionally to brighten their lives.

Table 10. Characteristics of a Borderline Personality Disorder, as indicated by at least 4 of the following:
1) a pattern of unstable and intense interpersonal relationships characterized by alternating extremes of idealization and devaluation
2) impulsiveness in at least two areas that are potentially self-damaging, e.g. spending, sex, substance abuse, shoplifting, reckless driving, binge eating
3) emotional instability: marked shifts from baseline to depression, irritability, or anxiety, usually lasting a few hours and only rarely more than a few days

(continued on next page)

4) inappropriate, intense anger or lack of control of anger, e.g. frequent displays of temper, constant anger, recurrent physical fights

5) recurrent suicidal threats, gestures, or behavior, or self-mutilating behavior

6) marked and persistent identity disturbance manifested by uncertainty by at least two of the following: self-image, sexual orientation, long-term goals or career choice, types of friends desired, and preferred values

7) chronic feelings of emptiness or boredom

8) frantic effort to avoid real or imagined abandonment.

From the Diagnostic and Statistical Manual of Mental Disorders, 3rd Edition, Revised (DSM-III-R). American Psychiatric Association

Religion

If borderlines are believing people, they relate to religion as they relate to most other things in their lives: being either totally involved or totally uninvolved. Just as a borderline's relationship with his or her family tends to blow hot and cold, so too does his or her relationship with religion and the Church. For a time, a borderline may be much involved in parish activities, only to withdraw completely from all contact with the church. Or, the pastor may be quite idolized as a substitute father and local hero, only later to become the object of rage because of some minor shortcoming or failure to live up to the borderline's expectations.

Image of God

The borderline's image of God reflects the volatility of his or her moods. In times of elation, God is kindly and beneficent, but when the borderline person is angry and depressed, God becomes a tyrant and the cause of the borderline's problems. People with a borderline personality disorder tend to blame everyone but themselves for their troubles. They direct their anger toward those they think caused their troubles, and God is no exception. They can harbor angry thoughts and feelings against God and the Church but are loathe to admit such thoughts and feelings to anyone else.

Pastoral Counseling

Due to their lack of trust, emotional instability, and turbulent style of relating to other people, borderlines are often some of the most difficult people with whom pastoral counselors have to deal. At first, borderlines will idolize the counselor, saying how much good he or she is doing for them and how much they appreciate the counseling. Then suddenly, for no apparent reason, the borderline's attitude changes. They begin to manifest negative feelings toward the counselor, complaining, for example, that they are not satisfied with their progress. Frequently, what has happened is that the counselor has inadvertently said something that the borderline has taken as a criticism, or the borderline has simply misinterpreted a remark the counselor has made. Consequently, counselors need to be careful in the way they present matters; at the same time, they need to realize that they are going to be misread, and when they are misread, they must be willing to clarify or correct what they have said.

Anger

Pastoral counselors should realize that the tendency of the borderline to be emotionally unstable and have angry outbursts can be disturbing. This is especially so if the counselor is not accustomed to dealing with angry, volatile people. For some counselors, overt manifestations of anger are intimidating and undermine the development of a good relationship with the counselee. Hence, when pastoral counselors sense that they are being intimidated by the counselee's intense anger, they should try to realize that the anger stems from the borderline's personality disorder, and not from anything they have done or failed to do, or from the person's dislike for them. The borderline person would manifest the same anger, no matter who was the counselor.

Avoiding a Negative Attitude

In dealing with borderline people, one of the counselor's most difficult tasks is to maintain a positive attitude and not become angry in the face of constant testing or clinging dependency, followed by angry, sarcastic remarks. Borderlines want the counselor exclusively for themselves, so they may test his or her willingness to cancel another appointment in deference to the borderline. Crisis-prone borderlines expect the counselor to be ready at all times to come to their assistance, even when the crisis is minor.[13]

Relating to the Counselor

Borderlines relate to the pastoral counselor in a way similar to the way they relate to anyone they meet for the first time. They begin relating in a friendly, cordial manner, but as the counseling session progresses, their behavior is apt to change abruptly. They are likely to begin testing the counselor to see whether he or she truly cares about them or is just going through the motions of being helpful and fulfilling his or her duty as a pastoral counselor. The testing may take the form of requesting an appointment at a time when the counselor ordinarily does not engage in counseling, or occupying the counselor in a long telephone discussion when he or she knows that the counselor has other obligations. Borderlines will often take as much of the counselor's time as they can get, up to two or three hours at one sitting, if the counselor allows. Consequently, counselors need to be firm in establishing limits early in the process. The counselor should give reasons for the limits, and at the same time show genuine concern about the borderline's personal welfare.

Unfortunately, borderlines have a history of terminating counseling whenever they take on a negative mood or become dissatisfied with a lack of progress. A tactic they sometimes use is to provoke such anger and frustration that the counselor feels he or she can be of no further help and so decides to end the counseling. Then the borderline feels justified: "I'm right. You can't trust anyone, not even dedicated Church people." When counseling borderlines, you should expect that some borderlines are apt to stop coming before their problem is resolved, and you should not blame yourself for the breakdown in the counseling process.

Making a Referral

Many borderlines may need some kind of psychiatric or psychological help, but often they are not open to such a referral. Some have previously undergone psychotherapy and do not want to begin the process once again, so it is wise to ask borderlines, before making a referral, whether they have been in therapy, for how long, and with what outcome. For any number of reasons, they may resist the suggestion that they seek treatment again. If a referral is made, they may not follow up on it. In general, people who do not want psychotherapy usually derive little benefit from therapy, so there is nothing to be gained by trying to persuade borderlines into accepting psychotherapy.

A good relationship with the pastoral counselor may be the reason for the borderline's accepting therapy. Moreover, it may pave the way for the psychologist or psychiatrist to whom the borderline has been referred to form a similar relationship with the person. However, the referring counselor needs to be on guard lest the borderline interpret the referral as a rejection. Pastoral counselors need to impress upon borderline counselees that the referral is being made because psychologists or psychiatrists have been specially trained to help people with problems like theirs and are thus more apt to be of greater assistance to them. At the same time, counselors should leave the door open for the person to return, if he or she wants to discuss some kind of a spiritual matter.

Since the psychiatric category of borderline is of recent origin, there is little long-term scientific research on the effectiveness of various treatments.[14] Initial clinical research seems to show that behavioral and cognitive therapies are somewhat more effective than psychoanalytic psychotherapy.[15] Therefore, a psychologist who has had some experience with personality disorders, and more specifically the borderline personality disorder, and has had training in behavior and cognitive therapy techniques should be given the nod over professionals trained in psychoanalytic psychotherapy, although the latter should by no means be excluded.

Psychotherapy with borderline personality disorders is seldom achieved in a matter of months but rather requires a couple of years or more. Therapists usually encounter great difficulty in trying to establish a trusting relationship with the borderline, a relationship such that he or she willingly cooperates with the particular form of psychotherapy being used and does not end the therapy prematurely. Moreover, having its roots in early childhood, the borderline personality is most difficult to modify. Medication usually plays either a limited role or no role at all in the treatment of a borderline disorder. However, if the borderline person has been depressed for a considerable period of time and therefore possibly in need of anti-depressant medication, then a psychiatric referral should be considered.

CHAPTER 10

The Schizophrenic Spectrum

PETER, AN ECCENTRIC, SINGLE, MIDDLE-AGED MAN LIVED ALONE IN a one-room apartment. As much as possible he avoided contact with other people. When going to the market—one of the few times he left his apartment—Peter was very self-conscious and felt that other people paid special attention to him. He thought that people sometimes crossed the street to avoid him.

Several months ago, Peter lost his job as a postal clerk because he frequently missed work and his performance was poor. Previous to that time, he had seldom held a job for any length of time, even though he was bright and a college graduate.

Peter's mannerisms were strange. He frequently spoke in a vague and abstract manner, and sometimes missed the point in a conversation. While talking about the various things that concerned him, he described his daily routine in elaborate and irrelevant detail. On one occasion he told how he had spent an hour in a pet store comparing two brands of fish food, reading and rereading many times the labels and directions on each item. Unable to make up his mind which to buy, he had left the store without buying either.

He worried that his angry thoughts about his brother and sister might harm them. At the same time, he was convinced that they were conspiring to get him out of their lives, whereas the truth was that both were very solicitous about him and his condition but at a loss as to how to help him.

The case of Peter is an example of an individual with a schizotypal personality disorder, which is a disorder related to schizophrenia both in its name and its similar characteristics. Along with the schizoid and paranoid personality disorders, the schizotypal is at the least-severe end of the spectrum of schizophrenic disorders, while the disoriented, hospitalized schizophrenic in the acute phase of a psychotic breakdown is at the most severe end. Like the borderline, the schizotypal personality disorder is a relatively new psychiatric classification, with only limited research to substantiate its existence and characteristics. Formerly, people with this disorder were classified as borderline schizophrenics or simple schizophrenics.

The Schizotypal Disorder

Individuals with a schizotypal personality disorder are strikingly odd and strange in their way of thinking, perceiving, and speaking, and their peculiar behavior sets them off as different. Yet these characteristics are not severe enough to warrant a diagnosis of schizophrenia.[1] More recent research suggests that isolation from other people, excessive concern over health, and being overly suspicious are the most useful indicators of this personality disorder.[2]

The disheveled man who appears at the rectory door, asks for a handout, and whose speech is difficult to follow is likely to fall into the classification of schizotypal. Many of the people who live on our city streets or in "flop houses" have this type of disorder. Occasionally, a schizophrenic whose disorder is in remission is classified as schizotypal.[3]

Characteristics

Schizotypals are usually eccentric in the way they act, unkempt in appearance, and socially withdrawn. "Because of their more advanced state of pathology, schizotypals frequently lead a meaningless, idle, and ineffectual existence, drifting from one aimless activity to another, remaining on the periphery of societal life, and rarely developing intimate attachments or accepting enduring responsibilities."[4]

Often they are given to strange beliefs, magical thinking, and the occult. Sometimes they believe that they have access to the minds of other people and can influence the way these people think and act. Some schizotypals claim to be clairvoyant or to have mental telepathy. Others feel that they are not human or exist outside their bodies, "watching themselves" move through life.

Behavior

People with the schizotypal disorder are aloof and live much of the time within themselves. They are unaware of their own feelings but very sensitive to the feelings of others, especially to any sign of anger.[5] Few things in the world stimulate their interest or bring them pleasure. They are detached and uninvolved observers, watching the passing scene go by. Sometimes they are "pack rats," collecting all kinds of useless items, such as old newspapers, magazines, or various tools and fixtures. They can spend hours at a time arranging these items.

Thought Patterns

"While social isolation, constricted or inappropriate affect, and unusual behavior are characteristic of a schizotypal personality disorder, the most striking features are oddities of cognition. The cognitive distortions in this disorder are among the most severe of any in the personality disorders."[6] Their speech is tangential, circumstantial, vague, and overelaborated. Although gross thought disorder is absent, the meaning of their speech may require interpretation. Schizotypal people believe that they have special powers of thought and insight, and frequently are overly suspicious and quick to misjudge others, as exemplified by Peter's belief that his sister and brother were conspiring against him when they actually were trying to help him.

Table 11. Characteristics of a Schizotypal Personality Disorder, as indicated by at least 5 of the following:
1) excessive social anxiety, e.g., extreme discomfort in social situations involving unfamiliar people;
2) odd beliefs or magical thinking influencing behavior and inconsistent with subcultural norms, e.g., superstitiousness, belief in clairvoyance, telepathy, or "sixth sense";
3) unusual perceptual experiences, e.g., illusions, sensing the presence of a force or person not actually present;
4) odd or eccentric behavior or appearance, e.g., unkempt, unusual mannerisms, talks to self;
5) no close friends or confidants (or only one) other than first-degree relatives;
6) odd speech, e.g., speech that is impoverished, digressive, vague, or inappropriately abstract;
7) inappropriate or constricted affect, e.g., silly, aloof, rarely reciprocates gestures or facial expressions, such as smiles or nods;
8) suspiciousness or paranoid thinking.
From the Diagnostic and Statistical Manual of Mental Disorders, 3rd Edition, Revised (DSM-III-R). American Psychiatric Association

Schizophrenia

People with schizophrenia are at the opposite end of the schizophrenic spectrum. Their symptoms are usually much more severe and debilitating than are those of the schizotypal person. Schizophrenics are classified as psychotic rather than as having a personality disorder. Schizophrenia accounts for over half of the people in the U.S. who suffer from a psychosis. Its major characteristics are 1) withdrawal, 2) disorganization of the thought process, 3) disturbances in emotions and affective life, 4) disorientation as to time, space and person, 5) severe impairment of social and personal functioning, 6) inability to perform the usual household and occupational roles, and, in some cases, 7) bizarre behavior, hallucinations and delusions. In the acute phase, a chief characteristic of schizophrenia is withdrawal from reality and living in a world of his or her own making.

While there is yet no definitive evidence, research leads us to conclude that schizophrenia is a disorder of the brain that results from a chemical imbalance.[7] As yet no physical features of the brain have been unequivocally associated with the specific symptoms of schizophrenia. Research also indicates that schizophrenia runs in families. For this reason it is thought by some to be, at least in part, genetic in origin.[8]

Case of Miss H.

The following case describes a schizophrenic woman with religious delusions who might possibly seek the help of a pastoral counselor.

Miss H. is a 39-year-old woman with a long psychiatric history who arrives at the emergency room in the middle of the night seeking hospitalization. She is no stranger to the hospital staff and is well-known for her cowgirl outfits and bizarre tales. During the past several years, she has arrived at the hospital every few months with a new story of woe. Her stories often warrant admission, and they always elicit sympathy.

The history is well-documented in her lengthy chart. Miss H. has had auditory hallucinations more or less continuously for 22 years. The voices are those of pleasant female companions, strangers who have died but now cannot make it to heaven. Miss H. believes that God has chosen her to comfort these lost souls and to convey their messages to those who are still on earth.

From time to time she journeys to Times Square to fulfill this duty. She finds few listeners but, not easily discouraged, she takes consolation in the conviction that her thoughts are being transmitted via television to those who are not yet receptive to a more personal approach. She worries only that the transmissions might be intercepted by powerful messengers representing a malevolent force. Unless she is extremely cautious, this "counter-power" could influence her thoughts and force her to behave strangely.

Since her family wants nothing to do with her, Miss H. has spent long stretches of her life in custodial hospitals. In recent years, she has spent increasingly longer periods of time out of the hospital while being maintained on low-dose phenothiazine. The medication helps her feel more relaxed but, even when pushed to extremely high doses, this has not been helpful in reducing her hallucinations, delusions, or thought-broadcasting. For the past several months, she has been living in a foster-care placement with two former inpatients. She has been spending her weekdays at a low-intensity day hospital, where she bakes cookies, crochets, and, to the delight (or at least tolerance) of all, leads the afternoon square dancing. Normally, this living arrangement seems quite satisfactory, although she finds the weekends boring—unless she makes her occasional sojourn into the streets to do God's work."[9]

Miss H. has many of the characteristics of a person with schizophrenia whose disorder is somewhat in remission. Most of the time she is able to function outside of a hospital. Because her delusions are of a religious nature, she is someone who might come to a parish rectory to seek help. "Schizophrenia has a vast range of symptoms, from aimless agitation to total immobility, from apathy and social withdrawal to bizarre delusions, hallucinations, and incoherent thinking. These symptoms come and go unpredictably."[10]

Positive and Negative Symptoms

The symptoms of schizophrenia may be either positive or negative.

Patients whose illnesses are dominated by positive symptoms are conspicuous, disturbing to others, and easily identifiable. They are subject to bizarre delusions of persecution; hallucinatory voices issuing insults and commands; inappropriate laughter and tears; sudden senseless rages; incoherent wandering speech and think-ing; and disconcerting erratic behavior. They are psy-chotic—unable to test the reality of their thoughts and perceptions.

Patients with an illness dominated by negative symp-toms have toneless voices and expressionless faces. They make few gestures or spontaneous movements. They avoid eye contact and rarely smile or return greetings. They speak infrequently, slowly and hesitantly; what speech they do produce is empty and obscure. They often lose a thought in the middle of a sentence, as though it had been removed from their minds; this is known as thought-blocking. They are unable to concen-trate, initiate activity, or even take much pleasure or in-terest in anything.[11]

Delusions and Hallucinations

Delusions and hallucinations are the most significant indi-cators of a psychotic condition and best distinguish the schizo-phrenic from the schizotypal.[12] Delusions are false beliefs that the person refuses to change, even in the face of contrary evid-ence. Miss H's belief that she was in contact with people in the next life and had a mission to save people in this world from going to hell is an example of a delusional system.

There are four types of delusions: 1) grandeur, 2) persecution, 3) guilt and sin, and 4) religious. Miss H.'s delu-sion is called a delusion of grandeur because she envisions her-self as God's special envoy to preach salvation to people before it is too late. Sometimes people with delusions of grandeur go even further and maintain that they are very important person-ages, such as Jesus Christ or the Blessed Virgin.

Delusions of Persecution

People who suffer from delusions of persecution are con-vinced that another person or group of persons hate them and are about to harm them, even though there is little or no justification for thinking this way. An example can be seen in the man who some years ago visited his parish priest to complain about the Communists in Moscow who were trying to steal an electronic device which he had invented and which was not yet known to other scientists. He said the Communists had access to his brain through electrical currents, and so he had to be on his guard whenever he was around electric wires. After reporting this to the counselor, he began looking around the room to see if there were any exposed electric wires.

Sin and Guilt

Sin and guilt can also be the basis of delusions. In this case, the person is convinced that he or she has committed a terrible, unforgivable sin, even though there is little or no reason for the person to feel this way. As a consequence, the person often loses all self-respect, feels worthless, and loses hope of personal salvation.

Schizophrenics may also suffer from religious delusions, such as thinking the end of the world will occur on a certain day or that they have been chosen by God to establish a new spiritual era. They may believe that they are possessed by the devil, and even able to feel the devil's presence near them. Because schizophrenics are convinced of their delusions, they usually cannot be "talked out of" them, and thus, they see no reason to consult a psychiatrist. Some say they can be helped only by a priest who is capable of giving them spiritual guidance.

Hallucinations

Hallucinations are perceptions that occur in the absence of a stimulus, and can be either auditory or somatic. Auditory hallucinations entail hearing voices either from within the afflicted person's head or from the outside. Schizophrenics may hear two or more people conversing or several people mumbling something that is hardly audible; often they think that these voices are talking about them in a derogatory way.[13] They may also believe that their thoughts are heard or controlled by others and sometimes even broadcast to the rest of the world through some kind of an electronic device.

Somatic hallucinations refer to strange sensations experienced in different parts of the body, with no internal stimulus or disorder to account for these feelings. The woman who feels that a knife is buried deep in her brain or the man who feels his liver rotting are examples of somatic hallucinations.

Beginning Signs

Schizophrenia usually begins in late adolescence or early adulthood. Early symptoms include tenseness, inability to concentrate, insomnia and social withdrawal. These are followed by peculiar behavior, nonsensical talk, and unusual perceptions, such as the person thinking that his or her brain is exploding or emitting rays that penetrate the brains of other people.[14]

Acute Stage of Schizophrenia

The acute schizophrenic (usually hospitalized) lives in a world of his or her own making, cannot think rationally, links together words and phrases in an unrelated and bizarre way (loosening of associations), and frequently displays odd or repetitious behavior. Some schizophrenics repeat the same word or sounds over and over again or use words or phrases that have no meaning, while others hardly speak at all or become catatonic, maintaining the same rigid posture hour after hour.

Emotions and Feelings

Schizophrenia severely alters the afflicted person's emotional life and way of feeling, which can be one of the most distressing features of this disorder. Sometimes the schizophrenic's emotional reactions seem to be totally unrelated to the reality of the situation, as exemplified by the schizophrenic woman who manifests inappropriate giggling or laughing at a funeral or the man who reacts to a minor annoyance by a violent outburst of anger that astonishes the person whose innocuous remark prompted the outburst. Other schizophrenics display almost no feeling whatsoever and appear apathetic and lethargic, no matter how disturbing the situation. Restricted affect shows itself by the person's lack of vocal inflection, paucity of expressive gestures, poor eye contact, decreased spontaneous movements, or unchanging facial expression.[15]

Subacute Stage

After the acute psychotic breakdown, many schizophrenics settle into a subacute stage with some residual, but considerably less distressing and debilitating, symptoms of the previous stage. In this stage the person is more in contact with reality, may work, and even have some kind of a social life. The transition from acute to subacute is more likely to happen if the person is taking some kind of anti-psychotic medication and undergoing psychotherapy.[16] During the subacute period, schizophrenics may be withdrawn and apathetic, somewhat removed from reality. They may behave and dress in an eccentric manner, and neglect to care for personal hygiene and grooming, but make a borderline adjustment at home and socially. The pastoral counselor is much more apt to encounter the schizophrenic person during this latter phase of the illness than during the acute phase. Subacute schizophrenics may still have somatic and auditory hallucinations as well as some lesser delusions, but these occur less frequently and with less intensity. It should also be noted that some schizophrenics seem to become almost normal after an acute psychotic episode and manifest few, if any, of their former symptoms.

Religion

People with a schizotypal personality disorder and schizophrenia have both authentic religious experiences and religious experiences that are a consequence of their disorders. In trying to help schizotypals and schizophrenics, the pastoral counselor needs to determine what is authentic and what is the product of their mental disorder.

If the person indicates that he or she has a past history of mental or emotional illness, this should be taken into account in evaluating his or her religious experience and in determining whether the experience is a grace or a hallucination or delusion. But the counselor should always keep in mind that God can give special graces to psychotic people, and these people can cooperate with these graces.

Schizotypals and Religion

If schizotypals are religious people, they tend to follow fringe and out-of-the-ordinary religious beliefs and practices, and become involved in new and unusual movements in the Church. Sometimes they may also believe that they have exceptional spiritual powers, such as being prophetic, having heightened psychic powers, and the power to heal. On the other hand, it is not unusual for schizotypal people to abandon the religion of their upbringing and convert to a cult, a fundamentalist Christian group, Zen Buddhism, or the Hari Krishnas.

Due to their uneasiness around people and their awareness of attracting attention by being different, schizotypals are likely to avoid crowded churches or other situations where they may have to contend with a large number of people. If they go to church, they are likely to be found in the back pews and at early services, when the congregation is usually small. Due to their appearance and behavior, schizotypals often stand out in a congregation. Even though they may not manifest it, schizotypals are very aware that they are different and sensitive to ridicule. On the other hand, they are most appreciative of anyone who reaches out to them and includes them in the parish community.

Schizophrenics and Religion

Many schizophrenics have religious experiences; some of these stem from their mental disorder and others from grace. If the schizophrenic was a devout person before becoming ill, his or her hallucinations and delusions are more apt to center on religious themes and symbolisms. For instance, a schizophrenic woman may experience the actual physical presence of Christ while at church; or she may hear the voice of God speaking to her as she is taking her daily walk. At another time, she may awaken from sleep to hear Satan moving around in her closet; she may then feel encompassed by evil and under the power of Satan. Some schizophrenics are convinced that they are uniquely called by God to a special mission, and that they must answer this call, no matter what it costs. The voice or voices that schizophrenics hear are often unintelligible, yet schizophrenics try to give some meaning to the sounds they hear. If the schizophrenic is a spiritual person, he or she is liable to interpret these as God or Satan speaking.

Ideas of Reference

While listening to a homily or sermon on sin and evil, some schizophrenics think that the speaker has access to their minds, "sees" into their souls, sees their sins, and then addresses the sermon or homily directly at them. Not surprisingly, other schizophrenics think that they can put ideas into the speaker's mind, and therby control what the homilist says. This psychic phenomenon is called having ideas of reference.[17]

Their disorder causes some schizophrenics to interpret pathological sensations as a religious experience. For instance, a schizophrenic woman took a piercing sensation within her chest to be an arrow of Christ's love penetrating her heart. Another schizophrenic woman, convinced that the statue of the Blessed Mother had moved, spoke to it while she was at Mass; and a schizophrenic man believed that he saw Christ in the host at the time of the elevation.

Ecstasies

Sometimes schizophrenics claim they have had an ecstasy, when most probably what they have had is an "out-of-body experience." This psychic phenomenon, in which the person feels that he or she is outside of his or her body, can be explained by natural causes. Still others maintain that Christ or the Blessed Mother have spoken to them and have given them a special message. In light of these individuals' psychotic history, these experiences are probably the product of a schizophrenic mind.

Pastoral Counseling with Schizotypals

Pastoral counselors should approach counseling with schizotypals as they would with any other parishioner, keeping in mind that people with this disorder have a number of handicaps which can affect the counseling process as well as the way they view reality.

First of all, when counseling schizotypals, counselors should be aware of the difficulty these people have in relating to others. Schizotypals want to relate to others but their fear of being ridiculed or rejected keeps them from doing so. It is difficult for schizotypals even to consider seeking counseling because of their fear that the counselor may ridicule or reject them. Thus, the counselor's first task is to try to form a good relationship by being affable, kind, and accepting. Any signs of annoyance—at the person's odd behavior, strange mode of dress, peculiar mannerisms, or unusual way of speaking—can militate against forming the kind of working relationship necessary for any hope of success in counseling. What schizotypals need is unconditional acceptance, even in the face of their being different from other people, and an indication that the counselor is genuinely interested in trying to help them.

During the counseling sessions, schizotypal people may give little indication that they are in touch with the counselor. Frequently, they will make little eye contact, have limited facial expression, and speak in a flat tone of voice. The schizotypal's mistrust of others and low self-esteem are at the root of his or her lack of contact with the counselor. Anything counselors can do to offset this mistrust and enhance the person's self-esteem will facilitate progress and ultimately lead to a more successful outcome.

Counseling, a Threat

Schizotypal people are often reclusive and seldom associate with others. Seeing a pastoral counselor demands that they get in contact with another person and talk with him or her on a personal level, which can be extremely threatening to schizotypals. As a consequence, they rarely seek counseling or psychotherapy on their own. If they do, it is usually at the urging of a parent, brother, sister or friend, and often in a time of crisis. To counteract the schizotypal's fear of people, it is imperative that the counselor be friendly and outgoing. He or she should be prepared to do most of the talking, at least in the beginning. Spending time talking about the weather or inconsequential things and letting the schizotypal do the same can break the ice and promote a higher comfort level in the counselee.

Schizotypals tend to ramble and become enmeshed in numerous details and tangents. Once they get around to talking about what brought them to counseling, their language may shift to vague generalities that often lead nowhere. The counselor needs to focus the dialogue on the person's concern and repeatedly bring him or her back to this concern. In trying to control the schizotypal's wanderings, the counselor will need to use some basic counseling skills, such as focusing, clarifying, and summarizing.[18]

If the counselor does not understand what the person is saying, he or she should simply say so, and ask the person to explain the matter again rather than let it pass. If the counselee rambles on about a number of disjointed subjects, the counselor, on the grounds of not fully understanding, might ask the person to repeat what he or she has just said. If the person is unable to do so (which is likely), the counselor might suggest an issue that seems more central and will help to focus the dialogue on what brought the person to counseling in the first place. The schizotypal should not be allowed to wander, particularly if the counselor is not sure what the person is saying.

Schizophrenics and Counseling

A schizophrenic is more likely to seek pastoral counseling during the subacute phase, when many of his or her symptoms are in remission, and not at the time of a psychotic breakdown, when overwhelmed with hallucinations, delusions, and emotional turmoil. During the subacute stage, a number of the symptoms of the breakdown stage remain but to a lesser degree. Especially during an initial session, the individual may even appear quite normal. Not infrequently the person makes at least a minimal adjustment to the world of work, family, and friends.

In trying to help schizophrenics, pastoral counselors should not assume the role of a psychiatrist or psychologist. They have not been trained to analyze the counselee's disordered thinking and behavior; moreover it is almost certain that schizophrenia has a physiological basis and calls for a chemical solution. Furthermore, research shows that psychological analysis is seldom helpful and can even be confusing and harmful.[19] Amelioration of the disorder usually requires medication, such as Thorazine (chlorpromazine), Stellazine, or most recently, Clozapine, all of which have a chemical effect upon the defective brain cells.

Assuming that the person is under the care of a psychiatrist and on medication, the pastoral counselor's main task is to offer encouragement and emotional support. Such support may help the person resolve the problem that brought him or her to counseling. At times, a pastoral counselor may need to help the person distinguish what is a valid religious experience from what is the result of schizophrenia. All things considered, it is probably best that pastoral counselors deal with schizophrenics as they would with any other counselee, i.e., working around any of the symptoms the person may manifest but at the same time keeping in mind how schizophrenia can seriously alter a person's way of thinking and feeling. Sometimes, it can be helpful to point out to the schizophrenic person that there could be another way of looking at what they experience. Counselors should not argue if the schizophrenic rejects the suggestion.

When dealing with paranoid schizophrenics whose psychotic disorder is in remission, there is little value in arguing with them about the lack of validity of their delusions, as in the case of the paranoid man who was convinced that his neighbor was stealing tools from his garage when, in fact, the neighbor had not stolen anything. It is good to remember that delusions are a part of the schizophrenic's real world which he does not want to relinquish. Delusions are his means of defending against his feelings of inadequacy and worthlessness.

Things to Remember

Schizophrenics often find relating to others extremely difficult. This is so especially during periods of withdrawal, because, like schizotypals, they fear rejection. Often it is with these feelings that the schizophrenic approaches pastoral counseling. As a consequence, the initial task of the counselor is to try to break down the wall between himself or herself and the counselee by being friendly, affable, accepting, and understanding.

Most schizophrenic people are convinced that their perceptions are not misperceptions but true to reality. When they hear a voice, such as God speaking to them and giving them a mission, it is, indeed, God speaking to them, so far as they are concerned. If the pastoral counselor immediately confronts the person with the dubious validity of this experience, the schizophrenic will probably reject the counselor's critical evaluation and withdraw further into himself or herself. If the schizophrenic is also paranoid, he or she will argue vehemently against the counselor's interpretation.

Schizophrenics are extremely sensitive to any kind of criticism. Only after the counselor has formed a good relationship with the person is he or she in a position to suggest that there might be other ways of looking at the schizophrenic's experience. Because of their disordered thinking, schizophrenics readily misinterpret what the counselor says, or not understand it at all. Also, the counselor needs to be aware that sometimes the schizophrenic's overt emotional reactions are not true to the way he or she actually feels. During a counseling session, schizophrenics can cry when there is no reason to cry and they do not mean to cry, and laugh when there is neither reason nor intent. So the counselor needs to question constantly whether he or she is truly in tune with how the person is actually feeling.

Schizophrenics need to be approached calmly, patiently, and gradually. Initially, the best thing the counselor can do for the person is to listen and try to be understanding, and then reflect back to the counselee how he or she must be feeling. Any challenge to what the person has said can quickly put an end to the dialogue or end up in a heated, useless argument.

Referral

In making referrals for schizotypals, counselors should bear in mind the difficulty of treating people with schizotypal personalities. Successful psychotherapy usually depends upon the psychotherapist's forming a good working relationship with the patient and then using this relationship as a springboard to bringing about change in the individual's personality and behavior.

Psychoanalytic psychotherapy, which encourages intense emotional expression and self-disclosure, can be very anxiety-provoking and, in the long run, counterproductive. Moreover, significant personality change, which is the goal of psychoanalytic psychotherapy, is unlikely. What schizotypals need most is practical advice and emotional support for their shaky self-esteem, which sometimes pastoral counselors can offer equally as well as psychiatrists or psychologists.[20]

Most schizotypals anguish over being cut off from other people and experience deep feelings of isolation. Consequently, they can be motivated to learn social skills so as to relate better to others. Behavior therapy has a number of strategies and techniques for learning new social skills or improving old skills, as well as modifying inappropriate behavior, so it is often the treatment of choice in making a referral.[21] If a referral is made, it should be to a professional who is able to offer behavior therapy. Usually this is handled by a psychologist, but some psychiatrists have also had training and experience in this type of therapy. Since medication is rarely used in treating schizotypals, the healthcare professional need not be a psychiatrist.

Schizophrenics

In treating schizophrenics, research shows that a combination of medication and psychotherapy has proven the most successful.[22] Some psychologists work with a psychiatrist in treating schizophrenics, but the more usual procedure is for a psychiatrist to handle both the medication and the psychotherapy. Therefore, people with schizophrenia are best referred to a psychiatrist, preferably one who has had considerable experience in dealing with schizophrenics.

CHAPTER 11

Depression and Personality

ONE EVENING SAM CAME TO THE PARISH RECTORY, OSTENSIBLY TO ask for information about becoming a priest. He said that several months ago he had quit his job as a sales manager in a prestigious company because he could not take the pressure and the long hours the job demanded, but that he now regretted the decision since he had been unable to find another job. When he was in eighth grade, he said, he had wanted to enter the seminary but his parents thought he was too young.

Twenty-six years old, Sam was the oldest of three children. He still lived at home with his mother and two sisters, ages 20 and 24. Two years before, Sam's father was killed while having coffee in a local restaurant. Even though there were no suspects, authorities thought the murder was related to drug trafficking. Sam's father was an alcoholic who physically abused his mother. Occasionally, Sam would fight with his father while trying to protect his mother, with whom he sided when his parents argued. He harbored a hatred for his father, had conflicting feelings about his father's murder, and felt guilty about the way he felt about his father.

As Sam talked, he gave the impression of being down, speaking in a low, submissive voice, with little animation. He told how he had attended a small suburban high school, graduated at the top of his class, received a number of honors, and then gone on to a large prestigious university. He did not do as well as he could have in college, but he did well enough to be admitted to a master's program in business administration in another school. After receiving his master's degree, he

135

got a middle management job in a local business where he initially did well. But gradually, as the pressure and long hours became too much for him, he began to question his ability to succeed in the business world. Frustrated and worried about himself and his future, Sam became exhausted and lapsed into a state of depression. He was unable to sleep at night, and frequently woke up in the early hours of the morning. He had difficulty getting back to sleep. Then he found himself not getting up on time and being late for work. Each morning he awoke depressed and dreaded facing another day. He began to isolate himself from his family, seldom saw his friends, and finally, in a moment of desperation, quit his job without giving his employer any notice.

What is a Depression?

Sam's way of thinking, feeling and behaving is typical of a person suffering from a depression. A depression is a state of mind which causes people to feel sad, low, despondent, and gloomy, or sometimes empty and devoid of any feeling.[1] Depressed people say they no longer enjoy things the way they used to and complain that life seems to have no meaning. They feel tired much of the time, and grumble about their not having energy to do much of anything. Sleeping is a problem for them. Often they wake up in the early hours of the morning and are unable to get back to sleep; or they have the opposite reaction, sleeping as much as 20 hours a day. Arising in the morning is the worst time of the day, but toward evening their life feels somewhat better. They lose interest in their work, family, friends, and sex. Eating becomes a problem: either they do not feel like eating or they eat too much. They complain of poor health; some of the complaints are real but many are imagined. They can be restless and agitated, or the opposite, listless and lethargic.

Thinking and Reasoning

A depression also disrupts an individual's mental abilities. People who are depressed are often unable to concentrate.[2] Their thinking slows down, and they complain of being unable to do mental tasks as rapidly as formerly. For example, paying one's monthly bills can take the depressed person as much as a couple of days, whereas before the onset of the depression he or she paid all these bills by mail on a Sunday afternoon. As a consequence, depressed people dread any task that calls for mental acumen, and put off such tasks as long as possible. If depressed individuals have to make a decision, they vacillate between alternative solutions. Often they fail to arrive at any decision. When they do make a decision, they frequently err because they are unable to see all the factors involved in the situation; they tend to look only at its negative side, and thus do not see the more positive options open to them.

Negative Attitude

The depressed often have a negative attitude toward themselves and feel that they are worthless. Consequently, they are wanting in self-esteem and self-confidence.[3] Often, depressed people speak about themselves in a disparaging way, and will contradict you if you try to point out their strengths. It is not uncommon for depressed people to tell you that neither you nor anyone else can help them. They are beyond help because their situation is hopeless. They may have suicidal ruminations, thinking about hurting themselves or ways of doing away with themselves.

Reaction to Depression

Depression is a disorder that strikes twice as many women as men and is one of the most common emotional disturbances in the U.S. It afflicts millions of Americans every year.[4] People react to a depression in a variety of ways. Some consider it a spiritual problem and seek the counsel of clergy or a pastoral counselor. Such individuals think they are suffering from the "black night of the soul" or that their depression is punishment for their sins and can be taken care of by a confession. Others think they can handle the depression by themselves. They are convinced that if they just live their faith, they can "pull themselves up by their bootstraps" and overcome their depression. Still others fail to see that they are depressed, and never seek any kind of help. They think that they are simply "down" and will get over it in time, which sometimes happens but more often does not. Finally, other people seek pastoral help for some other complaint, such as scrupulosity or a conflict with a spouse, in which case it is up to the counselor to recognize the state of depression and act accordingly.

The following Table 12 gives a list of the common complaints of depressed people and the percentage of depressed people with these complaints.

Table 12. Symptoms occurring in hospitalized depressed patients

Symptoms	Percent of Patients
Reduced energy level	97
Impaired concentration	84
Anorexia	80
Initial insomnia	77
Loss of interest	77
Difficulty starting activities	76
Worrying more than usual	69
Subjective agitation	67
Slowed thinking	67
Difficulty with decision-making	67
Terminal insomnia	65
Suicide ideation or plans	63
Weight loss	61
Tearfulness	61
Movements slowed	60
Increased irritability	60
Feels will never get well	56

From *Depression: The Facts*. George Winokur. Oxford University, New York, 1981.

Causes of Depression

Depression can be the result of any of a number of different causes, such as a chemical imbalance due to organic disorder, one of the symptoms of a neurotic or psychotic disorder, bipolar or manic-depressive disorder, or reaction to a loss. Determining the cause of a depression and treating it is the function of a psychiatrist or psychologist; recognizing the depression, helping the person maintain his or her faith during the time of depression and cope with it in the light of the Gospel message is the task of the pastoral counselor.

Types of Depression

Dysthymia and cyclothymia are types of a depression that pastoral counselors are apt to meet. Dysthymia and cyclothymia are like personality disorders, although they are not classified as such. They seem to be less serious versions of a major organic depression and a bipolar disorder (manic-depression). People with dysthymia are chronically depressed. Much of the time they seem to be down, rather like the little man in the cartoon who goes through life with a dark cloud over his head. Dysthymic people are generally negative in their outlook, and they are apt to complain about many things that don't suit them or they don't like. They manifest the following characteristics: chronic pessimism, depleted self-esteem, multiple body complaints, and self-withdrawal.[5]

Cyclothymia

Cyclothymia is a less-severe version of a bipolar or manic-depressive disorder (which is a psychotic disorder characterized by rapid swings in mood and extremely debilitating symptoms), having none of the psychotic features of a manic-depressive psychosis. People with cyclothymia tend to alternate between highs and lows, with almost half experiencing depression as their major symptom. Cyclothymics are more likely to seek help from a pastoral counselor during the depressed phase than the manic phase.

> The life of a cyclothymic is very difficult. The cycles of the cyclothymic tend to be much shorter than they are in the bipolar disorder. The changes in mood are irregular and abrupt, sometimes occurring within hours. Occasional periods of normal mood and the unpredictable nature of the mood changes cause the patient a great deal of stress. He often feels "out of control" of his moods. In irritable, mixed periods, he may become involved in unprovoked disagreements with friends, family, and co-workers.[6]

Many of the social problems cyclothymics have are due to the chaos caused by their manic episodes. Cyclothymics often complain of marital difficulties and unstable relationships with others, and alcohol and drug abuse are common. They frequently change jobs, move from place to place, and may become involved in a number of different religions and cults. Cyclothymic people seldom achieve happiness or success.

Case of Cyclothymia

Peter was a 29-year-old car salesman, a moody person who fluctuated between high and low periods. Since the age of 14 he experienced alternating cycles that he called "good times and bad times." During a bad period, usually lasting from four to seven days, he overslept, lacked energy, confidence, and motivation. Then for no reason he could see, he woke up in the morning to begin a period of overconfidence, heightened social awareness, promiscuity, and sharpened thinking. At such times he indulged in alcohol to enhance the experience, but also to help him sleep. Occasionally the good periods lasted seven to ten days, but then culminated in irritable and hostile outbursts, which often heralded the transition back to another period of "bad" days.

As a car salesman his performance was uneven, with "good" days canceling out "bad" days. Even during his "good" days he sometimes became argumentative with customers and lost sales that appeared sure. Although considered a charming person in many social circles, he alienated and lost a number of friends when he became hostile and irritable.[7]

Reactive Depression

Another kind of a depression which pastoral counselors are apt to encounter is due to some kind of a loss, hence the term "reactive depression." A reactive depression is caused by an external situation or situations, such as the loss of a spouse through death or divorce, a job, or possessions that are especially meaningful to the individual.[8] Often there are several loss situations that combine to provoke a crisis and bring on a depression.

Post-traumatic Stress Disorder

Still another kind of a depression pastoral counselors are apt to meet is the depression due to a post-traumatic stress or stresses. A post-traumatic stress disorder occurs when an individual blocks out of awareness a past traumatic experience, such as terrifying wartime experience, or a severely frightening fire, hurricane or earthquake, or childhood sexual abuse or rape. The depression results from repressing the fear or anger experienced at the time of the episode. It usually cannot be dispelled until the person acknowledges and faces the past traumatic experience and the emotions he or she experienced at the time.

Bipolar or Manic-Depressive

In the bipolar or manic-depressive disorder, the person swings between a major depression and uncontrollable elation or mania. Bipolar or manic-depressives have periods of severe depression, accompanied by psychotic symptoms such as hallucinations and delusions, which often are followed by a period of manic behavior. The depressed periods occur more frequently than the manic or elated periods. If manic-depressives are faithful to a program of medication (usually lithium), their periods of depression or mania tend to be less severe, and more quickly followed by longer periods of relative stability. Some manic-depressives, however, do not respond to medication, and their lives are an endless round of extreme "highs" and "lows," with sieges of distressing psychotic symptoms.

Manic Phase

During the manic phase, manic-depressives are "on a high." They are elated, euphoric and ecstatic, and their minds are overly active.[9] They have an exaggerated sense of self-esteem, tend to be grandiose, and intrude into social situations in an inappropriate manner. They engage in almost constant activity, endless chatter, and indulge in bizarre behavior, such as dressing in an outlandish fashion or running around without any clothing. Often they are unaware that their behavior is out of the ordinary. In the manic phase, manic-depressives have difficulty sleeping and are often irritable and belligerent. They exercise poor judgment and go on buying sprees, collecting a variety of items such as clothes, tools and trinkets, which they will never use.

In a social setting, manics are headstrong, intrusive, and manipulative. They are sensitive to the vulnerabilities and conflicts within their own families or the group with whom they live, and tend to exploit these vulnerabilities and conflicts. They are irresponsible in their behavior, frequently feel compelled to test the limits of those with whom they live or work, and tend to alienate family, friends, and co-workers. Manic-depressives rarely seek counseling or therapy during the manic phase because they fail to see their behavior as unusual, no matter how bizarre it might be, and thus they do not think they need help. If they seek the counsel of clergy, it is sometimes because they feel they are called by God to fulfill some important mission for the Church, and they want the clergyperson to help them implement this calling.

After a lengthy manic phase, manic-depressives sometimes sink into a period of deep depression and withdrawal, when they manifest many of the symptoms listed above. Often the higher the euphoria, the deeper the depression. Family members usually find it easier to live with the manic-depressive during the depressed stage than the manic, but the individual manic-depressive finds the depressed stage a living hell.

Special Periods When Depression Occurs

The following are periods of life when some kind of a depression is more apt to occur: 1) immediately or shortly after the birth of a child; 2) at menopause or climacteric; and 3) during old age. Whether depression that occurs during these periods is of biological or psychological origin, or both, is disputed.

About 2% of women, after the birth of a child, become seriously depressed, have delusions, and remain this way for an extended period of time. Thoughts of wanting to harm their newborn infant and/or themselves, along with somatic complaints, irritability, suspiciousness, and obsessive concern about the baby's health are common.[10] Some of these women seem to be quite stable before having the baby but within days or a couple of weeks after childbirth become severely depressed, even to the point of contemplating suicide. Others have a history of psychological problems, and the birth of a child worsens their condition. In either case, when a woman with a postpartum depression comes for pastoral counseling, she should be immediately referred to a psychiatrist because she is at risk of harming herself and/or her baby and needs the kind of professional help that is beyond the expertise of pastoral counselors.

Menopause

Between the ages of 48 and 55, for a period of two to five years, women undergo a natural physiological change called menopause. At this time, their menses or periods gradually taper off and depression can occur as one of a number of their symptoms. Other typical symptoms are anxiety, dizziness, irritability, and insomnia. There is no agreement among researchers whether menopause is due to physiological changes or psychological factors, or both.

> Women who have invested heavily in childbearing and childrearing activities are most likely to suffer distress during the post-menopausal years. Concern about aging, loss of childbearing capacity, and changes in appearance all may be focused on the social and symbolic significance attached to the physiological changes of menopause.[11]

When a woman who is of the right age and appears to be menopausal comes for pastoral counseling, she should be asked whether she is under the care of a physician. If she is not, she should be encouraged to see her family physician since there are medical procedures to help her through this stressful period of her life. What menopausal women need is understanding and emotional support, with the assurance that their disorder is temporary and the distressing symptoms will cease in time.

Climacteric

At a somewhat later age, men may experience a condition somewhat similar to menopause, called change of life or climacteric. At this time, the man undergoes a number of physiological and psychological changes, such as a lessening of interest in sex and capacity for sexual activity. For some men, this can be very distressing. Also, the climacteric man begins to realize that his life is more than half over and becomes more aware of his mortality. He looks at what he has accomplished or failed to accomplish, and what he foresees the rest of his life may have in store for him. Since his experience is more psychological than physiological, pastoral counseling from the vantage point of his faith can help him confront some of the distressing issues with which he is struggling.

Depression in the Elderly

Depression among the elderly (once called involutional melancholia) begins in late middle-age and is three times more common in women than men.[12] Some of the characteristics of this type of depression are: 1) a general loss of interest, 2) worry, restlessness, and anxiety, 3) feelings of helplessness and hopelessness, 4) feeling worthless and guilty, 5) finding life empty and meaningless.

Some of the factors contributing to the depression are: 1) poor health, 2) loss of occupation, especially among professionals and high-level business personnel, and 3) awareness of the inevitability of death. Depressed elderly look at their past and may focus their attention on how they have failed, as well as their not living up to their own expectations of themselves and the expectations of others. If they are dissatisfied with their past life, they are prone to despondency and despair because they realize that they cannot turn back the clock and change the past. Depression in the elderly is often accompanied by much self-criticism and negative self-evaluation, or by fixing the blame for what has happened to them on others. The rate of suicide and attempted suicide is considerably higher among the elderly than in the general population.[13]

Religion and Depression

Depression obscures one's faith and interferes with its practice. Some depressed people lose all interest in religion, feel that God has abandoned them, or go so far as to doubt the existence of God or a world beyond the present one. Others attribute their depression to their past sins, and feel guilty about being depressed. Still others become angry with God and think God has treated them unjustly by sending them such an affliction.

At a time when depressed people most need God's help, they often find it extremely difficult, if not impossible, to pray. If they pray at all, their prayer is one of anguish, begging God to release them from the dark pit of depression. A feeling of hopelessness overwhelms them. They may even think that not even God can help them, so they say to themselves, "Why pray?"

Inertia is a characteristic of the depressed state. Depressed people often find that they are unable to make themselves do the simplest tasks, such as getting up in the morning, putting on their clothes, washing their faces, and brushing their teeth.[14] Therefore, it should not be surprising to find that a person suffering from a severe depression abandons all practice of his or her religion, even though he or she may have been previously very faithful to it. Many depressed people stay away from Sunday Mass or other church services because they do not have the energy to make themselves leave their homes.

Another characteristic of depressed people is the perception of life as empty and meaningless. At one time, religion may have been important, but with the onset of depression, religion loses much of its meaning for them. As one patient put it: "Life is but one big empty nothing." As a consequence, the practice of religion is often completely abandoned, but not without feelings of guilt for neglecting it, which, in turn, only increases the depression. Depressed people say to themselves: "If I were truly committed to what I believe, and if I prayed, I would practice my faith instead of neglecting it, and then I would not be depressed." Such thinking makes these people feel even more guilty and depressed.

Some depressed people tend to see themselves as sinful and worthless, which drags them down deeper into the pit of depression. They also tend to focus on the negative side of their religious belief, such as sin, damnation, and Hell, which further intensifies their anxiety and downward spiral.

Depression and Pastoral Counseling

Some people seeking pastoral counseling appear to be sad, but they are not necessarily depressed. There is a world of difference between being "down" and being depressed. The person who is "down" is temporarily sad, often because of a recent distressing event. One usually gets over being "down" in a few hours or a day or two, at most. The person who is depressed has symptoms other than sadness and gloom and usually has experienced these symptoms for a long period of time. A few questions dealing with the cause of the emotional state and the length of time the person has had it can help the counselor distinguish between the person's being "down" or being depressed. Other indicators that differentiate the depressed person from someone who is "down" are the depth of sadness, neglected manner of dress and grooming, slowness of speech, unchanging facial expression, and sometimes mental confusion.

Seeking Help

If a depressed person seeks pastoral counseling, he or she most likely comes at the urging of another person and for a reason other than the depression. People with a major depression seldom seek help of any kind because they see their situation as hopeless. Often they do not have the initiative and energy to get themselves out of their house to seek help. They need someone to push them into getting assistance. On the other hand, individuals grieving over some kind of a loss, such as the death of a spouse, a divorce, or the loss of their home in a fire, are much more likely to seek help because they see the need for assistance in the face of an overwhelming catastrophe. It should be noted that individuals with a reactive depression are more likely to seek the help of clergy or a pastoral counselor than a psychologist or psychiatrist, probably because it is easier to admit having a spiritual rather than an emotional problem.

From the person's circumstances, pastoral counselors should be able to distinguish between different types of a depression, so as to determine whether they should try to help the depressed individual or refer him or her to a psychiatrist. In general, individuals who are severely depressed for no apparent reason should be referred for psychiatric treatment whereas people with a reactive depression frequently can be helped by a pastoral counselor.

Cheering Up the Depressed Person

People who are "down" or in a reactive depression will often react positively to a bit of appropriately-placed humor or efforts to cheer them up, while those with a biological depression are apt to consider humor or other efforts to cheer them up as a lack of understanding or a sign of insensitivity on the part of the counselor. Consequently, joking or being humorous should be avoided in dealing with depressed people. On the other hand, the counselor should not be overly serious and somber but rather make a special effort to be somewhat upbeat and affable.

Many depressed people are prone to discouragement because they are unable to see any end to their depressed state. If you show any sign of similar discouragement, you simply increase the counselee's discouragement. It should be noted that it is very easy for a counselor to become discouraged when dealing with depressed people because of their stubborn clinging to negative views of themselves and the world. Buying into the depressed person's feeling of hopelessness only increases that feeling. Depressed individuals need to know that their depression is time-limited and will eventually dissipate, no matter how depressed they are at the moment. There is an end to the tunnel of despair, even though the person may not be able to see it at the time.

Crying spells during a counseling session are often a signal of depression, especially if there is little reason to cry. Counselors needs to realize that most people do not like to cry and are embarrassed by their crying. They would control their crying if they were able. The counselor should learn how to be at ease when people cry and not try to stop them or give the impression that crying is a sign of weakness. As a matter of fact, the depressed person often finds it helpful if the counselor gives him or her permission to cry. Crying can be salutary as a means of communicating the extent of one's inner pain, sharing this pain with another, and not keeping it bottled up within oneself.

Grief

Crying is one of the ways we express grief. It is a normal reaction that occurs after the loss of one's spouse, close friend, or prized possession. The period of grief after a catastrophe allows the person to mourn the loss, realize how important a role the person or thing played in his or her life, and finally reorganize his or her life so as to go on without the spouse, job, or home. The task of the pastoral counselor is to encourage the grieving person to talk about and cry over the lost object, so as to move through the grieving process and then move on with life. This process can take several weeks or a year or two, depending upon the significance of the loss.

At the time of a loss, some people never seem to go through the grieving process. An example can be found in the woman who loved her husband very much but was dry-eyed all through his funeral services, spoke about him with her friends with no sign of grieving and, for all practical purposes, acted as if he were still alive. This woman may be stonewalling her inner pain, only to have it return later when she encounters another loss somewhat similar, at which time she may have what appears to be some kind of a psychological breakdown. The task of the counselor is to help her confront the loss of her husband at the time when it occurs by getting her to talk about his death, how she feels now that he is gone, what he meant to her, and the pleasant and unpleasant times she had with him.

Grieving people often feel guilty, thinking they are responsible for the loss, e.g., the death of the loved one, or at least could have forestalled it if they had taken better care of him or her or acted differently toward that person, particularly around the time of the death. They may feel angry at the deceased person for abandoning them and ruminate about past hurts, which only increases their anger. It is not uncommon for grieving people to see someone on a crowded street who looks somewhat like the deceased person and think that the loved one has come back to life.

What the grieving person needs is empathetic understanding, which means that the counselor understands what the counselee is going through and accepts how the counselee feels, even when he or she expresses anger towards God or the deceased person. At such times, the counselor should indicate verbally to the bereaved person this understanding and acceptance. Once this is accomplished, then some reflections on the meaning of life and hope in the next life will have much more meaning for the bereaved person. The more you can get grieving people to talk about their sorrow, anger, and guilt, the more helpful you will be. Also, it should be remembered that just being present with a grieving person can help to dissipate grief. Sometimes, the counselor needs to say nothing, but simply listen and accept the person's sorrow.

Decision-making

People should be discouraged from making important decisions while in a depressed state because their view of the world around them is restricted. They are able to see and understand neither all the factors involved in a problem nor all the available options needed to make a good decision. They look at the world from a negative or pessimistic point of view, which warps their judgment. If a depressed person wants to make a major change in his or her life, the counselor should encourage that person to forego the decision until he or she feels better and is no longer in a state of depression. Their depleted self-esteem and self-confidence militates against decision-making, especially if there is any risk involved in making the decision.[15]

Often depressed people are unable to make a final decision and stick to it. They change their minds frequently. If a decision has to be made because the situation demands some kind of immediate action, the counselor may have to decide what should be done and convince the person to follow this decision, but this course of action should be taken only after the person clearly demonstrates that he or she is unable to make a good decision on his or her own.

Referral

In general, depressed people are best referred to a psychiatrist who is able to prescribe medication, such as lithium for manic-depressives, as well as handle psychotherapy. Research shows that a combination of pharmaceutical therapy and psychotherapy is the most effective treatment for most depressions (with the exception of the reactive depression).[16] For reasons of economy, sometimes a psychiatrist may handle the patient's medication and a psychiatric social worker or psychologist, the psychotherapy.

Often a pastoral counselor can take care of a depression due to loss, such as the death of a spouse or child. Occasionally, however, this kind of depression requires more intensive treatment, and then a referral to a psychologist is in order.

People who have a major depression, recurrent periods of depressions or a manic-depressive disorder need psychiatric care, not only to receive appropriate medication but also to be admitted to a psychiatric hospital, if there is a need.

CHAPTER 12

Resume

PASTORAL COUNSELING IS A SPECIAL TYPE OF COUNSELING IN which a person of faith tries to help individuals live according to the principles and values of their faith or solve their problems according to these principles and values. In any kind of counseling, the counselor attempts to help another person change his or her behavior or way of thinking and attitudes, make decisions, and cope with a variety of life situations. During the counseling session, the counselor encourages counselees to speak about their thoughts, feelings, and experiences, with the hope that they will come to a better understanding of themselves and their situation, and as a consequence be led to make needed changes in their lives. If there is a problem, the counselee is asked to consider possible ways to solve the problem, and then how to implement the way he or she has chosen.

Faith and Counseling

Pastoral counseling differs from other kinds of counseling, such as psychological, educational, or occupational counseling, insofar as pastoral counseling involves in some way the individual's faith in God and what God has revealed, especially through Jesus Christ, His Son and our Savior. Faith is more than adherence to a set of beliefs, such as one finds in the Apostles' Creed. It is an enduring state of the whole person that involves intellectual assent, willing, trust, relationship and commitment.

Our faith is constantly changing, beginning in early childhood and progressing throughout the adult years. Faith is not static but can become stronger or weaker, more clear or more obscure. Faith can become distorted, confused, a source of inner conflict, or almost entirely disappear. One of the functions of pastoral counseling is to make people more aware of their faith and the role it plays or should play in their lives. If there are distorted or erroneous beliefs, the counselor tries to correct these. If the person's faith is almost dead, the pastoral counselor tries to reinvigorate it.

Personality

In addition to their faith, people bring with them their unique personalities when they come for pastoral counseling. If the individual's personality is disordered, the disorder can have an adverse effect upon his or her faith and the practice of that faith, as well as on the outcome of the counseling session. One of the functions of pastoral counseling is to help those with a personality disorder live their faith and follow the message of the Gospel, even though they are afflicted with a particular personality disorder. Consequently, early in the counseling session pastoral counselors should try to determine whether the individual coming for counseling has a personality disorder, and whether this disorder is interfering with his or her life of faith. The counselor must then find strategies to counteract the adverse effects of the disorder. If the disorder seriously interferes with the pastoral counseling itself or severely disrupts the person's life, then a referral to a psychiatrist, psychologist, or marriage and family counselor is in order.

Personality Disorders and Their Impact on Faith

The following list summarizes the personality disorders named in *DSM-III-R*, with their major characteristics and how these characteristics impact on an individual's life of faith.

1) *Dependent Personality Disorder*

This disorder is characterized by dependent attitudes and behavior towards others as manifested by clinging behavior, compliance, lack of initiative, and becoming overly-attached to others for affirmation and security. It can cause a person to become dependent on God and church personnel in a psychologically-unhealthy way.

2) *Passive-Aggressive Personality Disorder*

The person with this disorder resents the demands and suggestions of others and reacts by "forgetting," procrastinating, and avoiding obligations and responsibilities. He or she may manifest this kind of behavior when in pastoral counseling or relating to church personnel at other times.

3) *Narcissistic Personality Disorder*

The essential features of this disorder are self-absorption, a persistent and unrealistic over-evaluation of one's own importance and achievements, and a need for constant, special attention and admiration from others. Frequently people with this disorder are so self-centered that they have little interest in or concern for religion, but when they are involved, they seek special treatment from church personnel.

4) *Histrionic Personality Disorder*

The essential characteristics are: rapidly-changing, shallow emotional reactions; the use of unusual actions, appearance, and emotional behavior to evoke and maintain the interest and appreciation of others; and a need for constant reassurance and immediate gratification. People with this disorder may use church groups to try to get the attention and appreciation they need. Their faith is often superficial.

5) *Schizoid Personality Disorder*

This disorder is characterized by social withdrawal and a lack of ability to form warm and empathetic relationships. People with this disorder are apt to relate to God and religion in a formal, structured, and cognitive rather than affective manner. They are uncomfortable in any kind of a church group and so are seldom seen at one.

6) *Avoidant Personality Disorder*
People with this disorder mistrust and fear other people, but long for acceptance and affection. They relate to God in a similar way, fearing God and His punishment. They sometimes place a psychological wall between themselves and God. They are uncomfortable at church group meetings.

7) *Antisocial Personality Disorder*
This disorder is characterized by a habitual disregard for social norms and rules, lack of guilt feelings when they break these norms and rules, and exploitive, dishonest behavior. People with this disorder use religion for their own advantage and are often inconsistent in the practice of their religion.

8) *Obsessive-Compulsive Personality Disorder*
People with this disorder are taken up with mental and interpersonal control; they lack flexibility and openness. As perfectionists, especially in regard to morality, they are obsessed with details, and struggle with decision-making. Their image of God is apt to be threatening rather than loving. They are excessively structured and cognitive in the practice of their religion and given to scrupulosity.

9) *Paranoid Personality Disorder*
This disorder is characterized by unwarranted suspiciousness, mistrust of people, and expectancy of deception. Paranoids mistrust God, and see God as threatening and punishing. Their practice of religion is formal and lacking in depth, and they tend to espouse conservative Church positions and cling to them with stubborn determination.

10) *Borderline Personality Disorder*
People with this disorder are characterized by rapid

swings in mood, tempestuous interpersonal relationships, and mixed feelings of love and hate, anger and elation, depression and guilt. They blow hot and cold in their relationship with God and the Church. Inwardly, they tend to rage at God and to blame God, but they seldom reveal their feelings to others. Their attitude toward church personnel ranges from admiration to disdain, depending upon their mood.

11) *Schizotypal Personality Disorder*
This disorder is characterized by peculiarities of thought, appearance, and behavior. Schizotypals are emotionally detached and given to self-absorption. Their "religious experiences" may be authentic or due to their disorder. They feel others will not accept them and so shun group situations.

12) *Mood Disorders: Dysthymia and Cyclothymia*
People with dysthymia are chronically depressed, pessimistic, petulant about many things, and overly concerned about their health. Those with cyclothymia experience rapid swings in moods but are depressed more frequently than elated. In times of depression, the depression can obscure their faith and cause them to lose all interest in religion. Sometimes, they may feel abandoned by God and even devoid of faith.

Conclusion

If pastoral counseling is to be effective, both the faith and personality of the counselee must be taken into consideration. If the personality is disordered, the individual's faith and the practice of that faith will likely be undermined in some way. In dealing with people who have a personality disorder, it is the task of the pastoral counselor to adjust his or her counseling to the particular type of disorder presented, so as to help the counselee live more fully his or her faith.

Endnotes

Chapter 1

1. "Personality and Personality Disorders." *The Harvard Medical School Mental Health Letter*, September, 1987, Vol. 4, No. 3, p. 1.

2. J.G. Grunderson, "Personality Disorders," in *The New Harvard Guide to Psychiatry*, by Armand M. Nicoli, Jr. (ed.), Harvard University, Cambridge, MA; 1988, pp. 337-338.

3. *Diagnostic and Statistical Manual of Mental Disorders* (3rd-Revised). American Psychiatric Association, Washington, DC, 1987, pp. xvii-xxii.

4. Walter M. Abbott, S.J., The Documents of Vatican II. Dogmatic Constitution Dei Verbum, No. 5. p. 111.

5. Avery Dulles, "The Systematic Theology of Faith: A Catholic Perspective," in *Handbook of Faith: A Catholic Perspective*, James M. Lee (ed.), Religious Education Press, 1990, 146-47.

6. Richard P. Vaughan, "Growing in Christian Faith," *Human Development*, Vol. 5, No. 3, Fall, 1984, p. 40.

7. Richard P. Vaughan, *Basic Skills for Christian Counselors*, Paulist Press, Mahwah, NJ, 1987, p. 32.

8. Sidney Jourard, *Self-Disclosure*, Wiley, 1971, pp. 27-33.

9. Vaughan, *op. cit.* 1987, pp. 40-41.

10. Richard P. Vaughan, *Basic Skills for Christian Counselors*, Paulist Press, Mahwah, NJ, 1987, pp.16-23.

11. *ibid.*, pp. 150-168.

12. J. G. Grunderson, *op. cit.* p. 337.

Chapter 2

1. Robert B. Ewen, *An Introduction to the Theories of Personality*, 3rd ed., Lawrence Erlbaum, Hillsdale, N.J., 1988, pp. 3-4.

2. Theodore Millon, "The Disorders of Personality," in *Handbook of Personality Theory and Research*, L.A. Pervins (ed.), Guilford, New York, 1990, pp. 339-340.

3. Theodore Millon, "Disorders of Personality," *DSM-III-R: Axis II*. Wiley, N.Y., 1981, p. 4.

4. Alma E. Guinness (ed.), *ABC's of the Human Mind*. Reader's Digest, Pleasantville, N.Y., 1990, p. 149.

5. Gerald L. Klerman, "Classification and DSM-III-R," in A.N. Nicholi, Jr. (ed.), *The New Harvard Guide to Psychiatry*, Harvard University, Cambridge, Mass., 1988, p. 79.

6. Peter Tyrer, *Personality Disorders*, Wright, Boston, 1988, pp. 33-34.

7. Harold I. Kaplan and Benjamin J. Sadock, *Clinical Psychiatry*. Williams & Wilkins, Baltimore, Maryland, 1988, p. 279.

8. Theodore Millon, "Personality Disorders," in *Encyclopedia of Psychiatry* (Vol 3), R.J. Corsini (ed.), Wiley, New York, 1984, pp. 15-16.

9. "Personality and Personality Disorders," *The Harvard Medical School Mental Health Letter*, Vol. 4. No. 3, September, 1987, p. 3.

10. J.G. Grunderson, "Personality Disorders," in *The New Harvard Guide to Psychiatry*, by Armand M. Nicoli, Jr., (ed.), Harvard University, Cambridge, Mass; 1988, pp. 338-339.

Chapter Three

1. *Diagnostic and Statistical Manual of Mental Disorders* (3rd ed): DSM-III-R, American Psychiatric Association, Washington, D.C., 1987, p. 359.

2. Theodore Millon, "Disorders of Personality," *DSM-III: Axis II*, Wiley, New York, N.Y. 1981, p. 107.

3. *Ibid.*

4. Aaron Beck, Arthur Freeman and Associates, *Cognitive Therapy of Personality Disorders*, Guilford, New York, NY, 1990, p. 286.

5. Millon, *op. cit.*, p. 108.

6. *Ibid.*

7. John A. Talbot, Robert E. Hales and Stuart C. Yudofsky, *Textbook of Psychiatry*, American Psychiatric Association, Washington, DC, 1988, p. 641.

8. Beck, *op. cit.* p. 293.

9. *Ibid.*, p. 294.

10. *Ibid.*, p. 295.

11. John G. Grunderson, "Personality Disorders," in *The New Harvard Guide to Psychiatry*, by Armand M. Nicholi, Jr. (ed.), Harvard University, Cambridge, MA, 1988, p. 355.

12. Millon, *op. cit.* p. 244.

13. Millon, *op. cit.*, p. 254.

Chapter 4

1. J. G. Grunderson, "Personality Disorders," in *The New Harvard Guide to Psychiatry*, by Armand M. Nicoli, Jr., (ed.), Harvard University, Cambridge, MA; 1988, pp. 344-46.

2. "Narcissism," *The Harvard Medical School Mental Health Letter*, September, 1986, Vol. 3, No. 3, p. 1.

3. Theodore Millon, "Disorders of Personality," *DSM-III-R: Axis II*. Wiley, New York, 1981, p. 167.

4. *The Harvard Medical School Mental Health Letter, op. cit.*, p. 1.

5. Grunderson, *op. cit.*, p. 344.

6. Millon, *op. cit.*, p. 167.

7. Aaron T. Beck, Arthur Freeman and Associates, *Cognitive Therapy of Personality Disorders*, Guilford Press, New York, 1990, p. 243.

8. Beck, *op. cit.*, p. 244.

9. Robert L. Spitzer, A. Skodol, M. Gibbon, J. Williams. *DSM-III Case Book*, American Psychiatric Association, Washington, D.C., 1988, pp. 265-66.

10. Millon, *op. cit.*, p. 139.

11. Grunderson, *op. cit.*, p. 358.

12. Beck, *op. cit.*, p. 142.

13. Millon, *op. cit.*, p. 142.

14. *Ibid.*

15. Grunderson, *op. cit.*, p. 350.

16. Beck, *op. cit.*, p. 209.

17. Grunderson, *op. cit.*, pp. 345, 351.

Chapter 5

1. *Diagnostic and Statistical Manual of Mental Disorders*: DSM-III-R, American Psychiatric Association, Washington, D.C. 1987, p. 339.

2. John G. Grunderson, "Personality Disorders," in *The New Harvard Guide to Psychiatry*, by Armand I. Nicoli, Jr., (ed.), Harvard University Press, 1988, pp. 343-344.

3. Theodore Millon, *Disorders of Personality*, Wiley, New York, 1981, p. 273.

4. Aaron T. Beck, Arthur Freeman and Associates. *Cognitive Therapy of Personality Disorders*, Guiford, New York, 1990, p. 274.

5. Millon, *op. cit.*, p. 273.

6. Beck, *op. cit.*, p. 259.

7. DSM-III-R, *op. cit.*, p. 351.

8. *Ibid.*

9. Beck, *op. cit.*, p. 257.

10. Millon, *op. cit.*, p. 298.

11. *Ibid.*, p. 273.

12. *Ibid.*, p. 296.

13. *Ibid.* p. 306.

Chapter 6

1. Benjamin B. Wolman, *The Sociopathic Personality*, Brunner/Mazel, New York, 1987, p. 128.

2. George E. Vaillant and J. C. Perry, "Personality Disorders" in *Comprehensive Textbook of Psychiatry/III*, Vol. II, by H. I. Kaplan, A. M. Freedman & B. J. Sadock, Williams & Wilkins, Baltimore, MD, 1980, p. 1579.

3. *Ibid.*, p. 1588.

4. Wolman, *op. cit.*, p. 128.

5. Wm. D. Barley, "Treatment of Criminal and Delinquent Behavior," Wm. H. Reed, Darwin Dorr, John I. Walker & Jack W. Bonner, W.W. Norton, New York, 1986, p. 184.

6. "Antisocial Personality Disorder—Part I," *The Harvard Medical School Mental Health Newsletter*, July, 1985, Vol. 2, No. 1, p. 3.

7. Charles F. Reed (ed.), *Psychopathology: A Sourcebook*. Harvard University Press, Cambridge, MA, 1958, p. 28.

8. Aaron T. Beck, Arthur Freeman & Associates, *Cognitive Therapy of Personality Disorders*, Guilford Press, New York, 1990, p. 150.

9. *The Harvard Medical School Mental Health Newsletter, op. cit.*, p. 4.

10. *Ibid.*

11. *Ibid.*

12. *Ibid.*

13. Wolman, *op. cit.*, p. 157.

14. Barley, *op. cit.*, p. 184.

15. Wolman, *op. cit.*, pp. 144-145.

16. John G. Grunderson, "Personality Disorders" in *The New Harvard Guide to Psychiatry* by Armand Nicoli, Jr., (Ed.) Harvard University, Cambridge, MA, 1988, p. 347.

Chapter 7

1. *Diagnostic and Statistical Manual of Mental Disorders*: DSM-III-R, American Psychiatric Association, Washington, D.C., 1987, p. 356.

2. John C. Nemiah, "Obsessive-Compulsive Disorder," in *Comprehensive Textbook of Psychiatry/III*, Vol. 2, (3rd ed), H. I. Kaplan, Arthur Freedman and B. J. Sadock, Williams & Wilkins, Baltimore, MD., 1980, p. 1511.

3. Graham F. Reed, *Obsessive Experience and Compulsive Behavior*, Academic Press, Orlando, Florida, 1985, pp. 4-5.

4. "Obsessive-Compulsive Disorder," *The Harvard Medical School Mental Health Letter*, October, 1985, Vol. 2, No. 4, pp. 1-2.

5. Gail Steketee and Kerrin White, *When Once Is Not Enough*, New Harbinger, Oakland, CA., 1990, p. 23.

6. Theodore Millon, "Disorders of Personality," *DSM-III-R: Axis II.*, Wiley, N.Y. pp. 226-229.

7. *DSM-III-R*, p. 356.

8. Reed, pp. 48-49.

9. *Ibid.*, p.47.

10. *DSM-III-R*, p. 356 and Nemiah, *op. cit.*, p. 1513.

11. Millon, *op. cit.*, p. 231.

12. Aron Beck, Arthur Freeman and Associates. *Cognitive Therapy of Personality Disorders*, Guilford, N.Y., 1990, pp. 313-14.

13. *The Harvard Medical School Mental Health Letter, op. cit.*, p. 1.

14. *Ibid.*, p. 4.

15. John Paul Brady, "Behavior Therapy," in Kaplan, Freedman and Sadock, *op. cit.*, pp. 2143-47.

Chapter 8

1. J. G. Grunderson, "Personality Disorders," in *The New Harvard Guide to Psychiatry*, by Armand M. Nicoli, Jr., (ed). Harvard University, Cambridge, Mass., 1988, p. 342.

2. *Diagnostic and Statistical Manual of Mental Disorders*: (3rd ed.) DSM-III-R, American Psychiatric Association, Washington, D.C., p. 337.

3. Theodore Millon, "Disorders of Personality," *DSM-III: Axis II*. Wiley, New York, 1981, p. 372.

4. Millon, *op. cit.*, pp. 380-81.

5. G. E. Vaillant and J. C. Perry. "Personality Disorders," in *Comprehensive Textbook of Psychiatry/III* (3rd ed.) Vol. II, Williams and Wilkins, Baltimore, MD., 1980, p. 1574.

6. Millon, *op. cit.*, p. 382.

7. W. W. Meissner, *Psychotherapy and the Paranoid Process*, Jason Aronson, Northvale, New Jersey, pp. 30-31.

8. Millon, *op. cit.*, p. 380.

9. *Ibid.*, pp. 382-83.

10. Vaillant and Perry, *op. cit.*, p. 1574.

11. Grunderson, *op. cit.*, p. 342.

12. Millon, *op. cit.*, p. 373.

13. *Ibid*, p. 382-83.

14. Vaillant and Perry, *op. cit.*, p. 1575.

15. Aaron Beck, Arthur Freeman and Associates, *Cognitive Therapy of Personality Disorders*, Guilford, New York, 1990, p. 119.

Chapter 9

1. "Borderline Personality Disorder, Part II," *The Harvard Medical School Mental Health Letter*, January, 1986, Vol. 2, No. 7, p. 1.

2. "Borderline Personality Disorder, Part I," *The Harvard Medical School Mental Health Letter*, December, 1985, Vol. 1, No. 6. p. 2.

3. John G. Grunderson, "Personality Disorders," in *The Harvard Guide to Psychiatry*, by Armand M. Nicoli, Jr., (ed.), Harvard Press, Cambridge, MA, 1988, p. 348.

4. Jerome Kroll, *The Challenge of the Borderline Patient*, W. W. Norton, New York, 1988, p. 43.

5. Edna G. Goldstein, *Borderline Disorders*. Guilford, New York, 1990, p. 44.

6. Kroll, *op. cit.*, p. 53.

7. Aaron T. Beck, Arthur Freeman and Associates, *Cognitive Therapy for Personality Disorders*, Guilford, New York, 1990, p. 189.

8. Goldstein, *op. cit.*, p. 41.

9. Goldstein, *op. cit.*, p. 49-50.

10. "Borderline Personality Disorder—Part I," *op. cit.*, p. 1.

11. Kroll, *op. cit.*, p. 46.

12. Goldstein, *op. cit.*, p. 30-31.

13. Beck, *op. cit.*, p. 191.

14. Marsha M. Linehan, Marian L. Miller, and Michael E. Addis, *Dialectical Behavior Therapy for Borderline Personality Disorder: Practical Guidelines in Innovations in Clinical Practice: A Source Book*, Vol. 8, p. 45.

15. "Borderline Personality Disorder—Part II," *op. cit.*, p. 1.

Chapter 10

1. Harold I. Kaplan and Benjamin I. Sadock, *Clinical Psychiatry*, Williams & Wilkins, Baltimore, MD, 1988, 284-285.

2. J.G. Grunderson & L.J. Siever, "Relatedness of schizotypal to schizophrenic disorders," *Schizophrenia Bulletin*, Vol. 11, pp. 532-537.

3. "Schizotypal Personality," *The Harvard Medical School Mental Health Letter*, May 1987, Vol. 3, No. 11, p. 2.

4. Theodore Millon, *Disorders of Personality*, Wiley, New York, 1981, p. 400.

5. Aaron T. Beck, Arthur Freeman and Associates. *Cognitive Therapy of Personality Disorders*, Guilford, 1990, pp 136-137.

6. Kaplan and Sadock, *op. cit.*, pp. 105-108.

7. M. T. Tsuang, S.V. Faraone and Max Day, "Schizophrenic Disorders," in *The New Harvard Medical Guide to Psychiatry*, Harvard University, 1988, pp. 286-287.

8. *Ibid.*, p. 288.

9. Perry Frances Clarkin, *A DSM-III Casebook of Differential Therapeutics: A Clinical Guide to Treatment Selection*, Brunner-Mazel, New York, 1985, pp. 108-109.

10. Kaplan and Sadock, *op. cit.*, pp. 112-115.

11. "Schizophrenia," *The Harvard Medical School Mental Health Letter*, June, 1988, Vol. 4, No. 12, p. 2.

12. Tsuang, Faraone, and Day, *op. cit.*, pp. 266-268.

13. "Care and Treatment of Schizophrenia," *The Harvard Medical School Mental Health Letter*, June 1986, Vol. 2, No. 12, p. 1.

14. *Ibid.*, p. 2.

15. Tsuang, Faraone and Day, *op. cit.*, pp. 269-270.

16. "Care and Treatment of Schizophrenia," *The Harvard Medical School Mental Health Letter*, June 1986, Vol. 2, No. 12, p. 1.

17. Tsuang, Faraone and Day, *op. cit.*, pp. 267-268.

18. Richard P. Vaughan, *Basic Skills for Christian Counselors*, Paulist Press, New York, 1987, pp. 72-103.

19. Tsuang, Faraone and Day, *op. cit.*, p. 277.

20. "Schizotypal Personality," *The Harvard Medical School Mental Health Letter*, *op. cit.*, p. 3.

21. *Ibid.*, pp. 1-2.

22. Kaplan and Sadock, *op. cit.*, pp. 118-119.

Chapter 11

1. Gerald L. Klerman, "Depression and Related Disorders of Mood (Affective Disorders)" in *The New Harvard Guide to Psychiatry*, Armand M. Nicoli, Jr., (ed.), Harvard University, Cambridge, MA, pp. 309-314.

2. Susanne P. Schad-Somers, *On Mood Swings: The Psychobiology of Elation and Depression*, Plenum, New York, 1988, p. 25.

3. Stanley W. Jackson, *Melancholia and Depression*, Yale University, New Haven, 1986, pp. 224-225.

4. Harold I. Kaplan and Benjamin J. Sadock, *Clinical Psychiatry*, Williams and Wilkins, Baltimore, MD, 1988, p. 139.

5. Klerman, *op. cit.*, pp 319-320.

6. Kaplan and Sadock, *op. cit.*, p. 158.

7. *DSM-III-R Case Book*, American Psychiatric Association, Washington, D.C., 1987, pp. 31-32.

8. Kaplan and Sadock, *op. cit.*, p. 146.

9. Klerman, *op. cit.*, p. 314.

10. Kenneth Reed, *Lectures in Psychology*, Warren H. Green, St. Louis, Missouri, 1985, pp. 175-177.

11. Kaplan and Sadock, *op. cit.*, p. 269.

12. Reed, *op. cit.*, 171-75.

13. Kaplan and Sadock, *op. cit.*, p. 510.

14. George Winokur, *Depression: The Facts*, Oxford University, New York, 1981, p. 6.

15. Klerman, *op. cit.*, p. 313.

16. *Ibid.*, p. 331.

Index